RAISING
children
in the  11th Hour

RAISING
children
in the 11th Hour

VICTORIA FISHER

CFI

AN IMPRINT OF CEDAR FORT, INC.

SPRINGVILLE, UTAH

ISBN 13: 978-1-4621-1050-6

Published by CFI, an imprint of Cedar Fort, Inc., 2373 W. 700 S., Springville, UT 84663
Distributed by Cedar Fort, Inc., www.cedarfort.com

LIBRARY OF CONGRESS CATALOGING-IN-PUBLICATION DATA

Fisher, Victoria Akselsen, 1976- author.
  Raising children in the 11th hour / Victoria Akselsen Fisher.
    pages cm
  ISBN 978-1-4621-1050-6 (alk. paper)
  1. Child rearing--Religious aspects--Church of Jesus Christ of Latter-day Saints.
  2. Church of Jesus Christ of Latter-day Saints--Doctrines. I. Title. II. Title:
Raising children in the eleventh hour.

  BX8643.C56F57 2012
  248.8'45--dc23

                    2012015817

Cover design by Erica Dixon
Cover design © 2012 by Lyle Mortimer
Edited and typeset by Kelley Konzak

Printed in the United States of America

10 9 8 7 6 5 4 3 2 1

Printed on acid-free paper

For the women who have mothered me:

My mom, Ingunn Marianne, the most
competent and patient woman I know

My grandmother Inger, whose
candor, wit, and analysis I cherish

My grandmother Erna, whose passion and
personality will sustain me always

It is better to be far apart but close
than to be nearby and distant.

CONTENTS

MORAL AGENCY

"You are to do the choosing here and now during this exciting and wonderful time on earth. Moral agency, the freedom to choose, is certainly one of God's greatest gifts next to life itself."[1]

Dieter F. Uchtdorf

M EET ELINA, FOUR YEARS OLD. SHE LOOKS LIKE Goldilocks and, just like her fairy-tale counterpart, she is, in fact, missing from home.

She must have left while I was submerged in laundry, but I don't know for sure how long she's been gone. I just know that when I asked her five-year-old brother, Isak, he did not know her whereabouts.

Calling her name, I walk from room to room, checking in every nook and crevice. And then I realize that Sadie, our docile Labrador, is missing too. And the leash is not on its hook.

From our porch I can see the length of our street in both directions, but no Elina. After I place ten-month-old Anja in her crib (screaming in fury since it is not nap time), Isak and I mount our bikes. Time is of the essence. Going by car would not take me down the alleys, pathways, and spaces Elina might have gone. But after one block, I have to take Isak back. He is just too slow.

With trembling fingers, I turn on *Blue's Clues*, place Isak on the couch, and give him the handset to our land-line, thankful he knows how to use it.

"I have my cell phone, so you can call, okay? I have to find Elina. If Anja cries, it is okay. She is safe in her crib for now."

With a quivering lip and tears in his big green eyes, he agrees to stay behind. He understands I have no choice. *I'm leaving the ninety-nine to rescue the one.*

Back on my bike, I try to figure out which direction to go. We have the bustling university campus on all sides of our little neighborhood. We walk and bike all around this area daily—no route is more familiar than another to my little girl. She could be anywhere. I close my eyes and try to *feel* where she has gone. I race down Garfield Avenue and onto Farmer Street. Without stopping, I shout to people I meet, "Have you seen a blonde, curly-headed girl with a yellow lab?" But they haven't, and with each Elina-free street, my panic grows, and I wonder if the next missing-child tragedy will be mine. Minutes tick by like hours. I approach the corner store just as two undergraduate women exit and start toward campus.

"Have you seen a little blonde girl with a dog?"

They shake their heads, but after I roll past them, one of them yells, "Wait! Was it a golden retriever?"

Close enough. "Yes!"

"We saw her about ten minutes ago. It looked like she was headed toward the elementary school."

After a mad spurt down James Street, I *see* her! She skips into view around the corner of the school (presumably having been to the playground). Her blonde locks are a bouncing halo that complete her angelic looks. Sadie obediently trots by her side, and Elina smiles when she sees me.

A dozen simultaneous emotions and thoughts get jammed in my throat.

"Why did you leave, Elina? And without telling me!" is what comes out first.

"I'm just taking Sadie for a walk," she explains, her blue eyes glittering with happiness.

My subsequent hugs, kisses, tears, and inevitable lecture on our walk home does little to enlighten her. Instead, she is indignant.

"I can't walk Sadie by myself? But it's not dangerous. I know how to look both ways before I cross the street, and I can find our house."

I'm going to have to pull out more stops, apparently, so I say, "I was afraid someone had *taken* you, Elina."

"But if a bad guy came, Sadie would just attack him."

By licking him to death? But it's no use criticizing Sadie's protective abilities. Elina is convinced Sadie will chew off the leg of any bad guy who even so much as looks in her direction. So this conversation continues in a small circle, until Elina finally gets to the heart of the issue:

"I want freedom, Mom. I want to be free."

It is not the first time she has said it. What did I expect? That this conversation would be delayed for another ten years? Come on! This is *my* child. Did I really expect to be able to hover over her?

In the end, I had to relent some of my powers (or watch as my restrictions unleashed the rebel in her). After careful consideration, I gave Elina the privilege to walk Sadie by herself. On two conditions:

1. Never leave the house without asking first.
2. Stay close enough to where you can still see our house.

"And if you break either of these rules, you will never be able to walk Sadie by yourself again. *Ever.*"

She understood and obeyed. She'd been given freedom within reasonable parameters. And I took heart that it had worked the night she reached out from the top bunk and wrapped her strong but skinny little arms around my neck, saying, "Thanks for giving me freedom, Mom!"

As parents we are constantly engaged in this balancing act between our authority (sometimes driven by our fears for them) and our children's freedom of choice. We want them to become independent and capable adults. We understand that they are free moral agents—that is, beings who are "capable of acting with reference to right and wrong."[2] But the generation we are raising in the Western world today includes some of the most supervised and acted-for children ever born on this earth, because of the precarious time we live in and the potentially devastating consequences of a wrong choice.

Kids are scheduled, their activities organized. We moms arrange their play dates, to which they are driven and often accompanied. They do not run errands to the store for us. They do not play outside the way we did as kids. They rarely have to negotiate their own surroundings without an adult. In many ways, they are not used to exercising moral agency, their "ability to make moral judgments and take action."[3] At least not the way kids did one or two generations ago. More parents than students attend freshman orientation on college campuses across America, and those parents have to be told "hither, but no further" and be sent home so the freshmen can be allowed to act for themselves.[4]

In contrast, this generation of children is the target of more marketing and extreme media (if I may call it that) than any other before them. They spend more time inside playing video games and watching television while eating a far poorer diet than we did a generation ago. They are bombarded by marketing, creating insatiable desires for products they don't need. Kids are exposed to an onslaught of questionable messages about ethics, body image, and gender roles. They are the victims of outright propaganda and view more violence and sexually explicit content than anyone should, even adults (in my humble opinion). They spend less and less time in outdoor play. They have but limited opportunity to practice problem solving with their peers.

What will this combination of lack of time spent making decisions in the real world and solving problems for themselves, coupled with a constant media stream of messages, do to their ability to get a handle on their adult lives?

We fear and worry about our children's physical safety, as we should, but in the process they often lose out on needed opportunities to practice making choices for themselves. And although most parents fear for their kids being outside by themselves unsupervised, too few parents fear the effects of the Internet, video games, and other media, it seems. Kids repeatedly sink to the bottom among entertainment options, and therefore what choices they do make for themselves often lack inspired sources when it comes to morals, work, and sound principles.

Today's kids are raised in a generation that will suddenly turn into teenagers and young adults who may or may not know what to do with their adult freedom. Will they suddenly find themselves free-falling? Will they get enough chances to make choices when they are young in settings that will encourage good judgment? Or will they still be moral agency rookies when they are young adults and the stakes are much higher?

This is parenting in the twenty-first century. And this book is an attempt at seeing just a few of the multiplicity of aspects and practices—many that are worrisome and some that hold promise—facing our children in this generation and therefore us as parents.

Moral agency is the first and operating principle in our lives. We get to choose—for good or bad—and so does everyone else around us. It governs all aspects of life.

I do not pretend to have all the answers. This is but a glance at aspects of childhood today, an introduction to some of the complexities parents face. I have gathered some facts and brought them to the table. However lacking this presentation may be, I hope and believe that these facts can affect our choices as parents for good and improve the outcome of our parenting as well as the childhood of our precious ones. Never forget that we parents have moral agency too, and armed with information, we can find the courage and strength to swim upstream.

We can allow our children to foster their independence and practice decision-making while setting some basic guidelines for our family life. In fact, I believe we can provide a better environment for this to happen by shutting certain influences out and lifting our children, our families, and ourselves away from the path of least resistance. Regardless of all the forces preying on our children, if we know the enemy, we can better prepare our children for their lives ahead.

This is written from the trenches by one of the lowliest soldiers in the struggle. May we all put up a good fight.

Notes

1. Dieter F. Uchtdorf, "Your Right to Choose the Right," *New Era*, Aug. 2005, 8.
2. Websters Revised Unabridged Dictionary, 1913.
3. *Wikipedia*, s.v. "Moral agency," accessed January 11, 2012, http://en.wikipedia.org/wiki/Moral_agency.
4. Martha Irvine, "Start of College Can Be Harder on Parents than Freshmen," USAToday.com, September 5, 2010, accessed October 29, 2011, http://www.usatoday.com/news/education /2010-09-05-freshman-coping-parents_N.htm.

VIDEO GAMES

"A man who dares waste one hour of time has not discovered the value of life."

Charles Darwin

"I like video games, but they are very violent. I want to create a video game in which you have to help all the characters who have died in the other games. 'Hey man, what are you playing?' *'Super Busy Hospital.* Could you leave me alone? I'm performing surgery! This guy got shot in the head, like 27 times!'"

Demetri Martin

NUMBERS GATHERED IN A 2008 STUDY REPORTED THAT "video games are played in 90 percent of American homes with children ages 8 to 16 and that the U.S. average playing time of four hours a week in the late 1980s is now up to 13 hours a week, with boys averaging 16 to 18 hours a week."[1]

Is this what childhood looks like in the twenty-first century? What about that *Calvin and Hobbes* childhood I so adore? The boy in the tree house, wearing the newspaper hat and pondering life's mysteries on the nature trail, where is he? Have his parents sedated him with hours and hours of screen games instead of making him shovel snow off the driveway "to build his character," as Calvin's dad used to put it? Is he no longer making duplicators and transmogrifiers out of cardboard boxes? Has his imagination atrophied and his cognitive development been arrested? *Say it is not so!*

I remember well that on November 11, 2011, I was on my way to pick kids up from school when I heard the following report on National Public Radio (NPR): "Here's today's stunning figure. The video game *Call of Duty: Modern Warfare 3* sold about 6.5 million copies the first day it went on sale. According to Activision Blizzard, which released the numbers today, that adds up to more than $400 million in sales in North America and the U.K."[2]

Frankly, my heart sank. And as the story continued, I got that trembling feeling and uneasy stomach that I always get when I fear for the future of mankind. As though this is literally the edge of time, and here I am trying to raise four precious young children in the eleventh hour.

The NPR report continued: "Other than *Call of Duty*, there has never been another entertainment franchise that has set opening-day records three years in a row. Life-to-date sales for the *Call of Duty* franchise exceed worldwide theatrical box office records for *Star Wars* and *Lord of the Rings*, two of the most successful entertainment franchises of all time."[3]

The American Psychological Association (APA) adopted a policy resolution in 2005 that called for a reduction of violence in video games and similar media.[4] This was based on documented "negative impact of exposure to violent interactive media on children and youth."[5] But clearly, the APA resolution has gone unheard where it matters.

The NPR story continued with a spokesperson for the *Call of Duty* franchise explaining with great enthusiasm that it is not just kids and young people playing these kinds of games anymore but also adults in their thirties, forties, and fifties. And with yet more effective marketing and new game features, more players are expected to sign on.

As I listened, I saw the vastness of America in the form of a big city, as if from an airplane—houses without end, suburb after suburb after suburb in a sprawling metropolitan web. And with my newly acquired X-ray vision, I saw people cocooned in the houses in front of large screens, engaging in games, killing each other, increasing the amount of aggressive behavior in children and young adults (which it truly does), as if designed by some great evil force.[6]

By the time I pulled up in front of the school, I was queasy. The kids got into the car, and we began to head home. I turned down the radio and managed to smile and utter a perky, "How was your day?" But all I could think about was how I wanted to get home and shelter the kids under the protective wing of our home, trees, and nearby nature trail.

My efforts to protect our home are not enough, because even if my children will be mostly sheltered from the effects of these (in my mind) brain-wasting games, I fear for this generation as a whole. I fear for my children, who will live, work, and make their way among those kids who have spent so much time playing such games as *Call of Duty*, *Grand Theft Auto*, and *World of Warcraft* (this is by no means an exhaustive list). And honestly, even if all American kids ever play is online Mahjongg and Farkle, the amount of time they spend is worrisome enough. Screens overshadow playing outdoors, interacting with family members, and learning to solve everyday problems.

Don't think I hate video games. I don't. I played *Super Mario Bros.*, *The Legend of Zelda*, and many other Nintendo games when I was young, and I confess I have many dear memories from playing these games. Perhaps some parents reading this do too. During the dark and cold winter months, my mom and I spent many happy hours traversing the worlds of *Super Mario* and *Zelda* in particular, including their sequels. My mom was a real power player too. I was so proud to report to friends when she had completed every level. Truth be told, she was better than I was.

So with that history and being the complete sucker for fantasy and fairy tales that I am, I nearly jumped out of my seat when I recently saw an ad online for a new *Zelda* game, complete with the hero Link, being released just in time for Christmas. I, who have absolutely lamented the entry of the Wii console into our house ever since I gave the go-ahead to get one, was ready to whip out the credit card and buy myself a Christmas present of incredibly time-wasting proportions, justifying to myself that the kids and I could play this together and what fun and bonding it would be. It took some time for the urge to settle, but in the end I resisted.

When I was a child, I often roamed freely in the woods. I played outside with friends unsupervised. I walked to school alone at age five. Playing video games, in my youth, was not the main staple. It was a temporary diversion, one usually reserved for bad-weather days when I had run out of reading material. My concerns for the effects of video games today have to do with the context of the games' existence in children's lives. I suppose my main objections to video games are (1) the waste of time, (2) their addictive nature (both 1 and 2 due to the "neverendingness" of the game designs), and (3) the effects on developing brains—to say nothing of the fact that people can live perfectly fulfilling and far more productive and creative lives without them.

The reason our family finally broke down and allowed a gaming console into our house at all is perhaps the same as many other families. Despite having sworn no Wii (or anything like it) would ever enter our house and compete with all the wonderful pursuits life has to offer, I soon found out that other families had them and our kids became the annoying visitors who only wanted to play video games when they came to visit homes that owned them, simply because that was their only opportunity to play. Our son began spending an awful lot of time over at a neighbor's house, unable to tear himself free from their screen and popping over there more than was courteous. I was embarrassed by this on the one hand, and on the other, concerned that I had no control over what they played. I realized that having it at home and being able to control the time spent playing as well as the types of games they played was in the end a better solution for our family. But in addition to that, I also considered our number-one family objective and goal, which is posted in several places throughout the house and reads:

Make a home where everyone is happy to be.

With Isak more eager to be across the street or at any other house where video games could be found, we realized as parents that one thing we could do to make our home a place where Isak was happier to be was to have a Wii. It was neither Christmas nor Isak's birthday the day my husband brought it home, having found a good, used one on Craigslist at a decent price. We had to tell Isak three times before he believed us.

"But you always said we would never get a Wii!" he exclaimed several times.

Well, my son, never say never.

We found that many of the Wii games are really fun, of course, and several allow for happy family moments, especially the sports games like bicycling that almost everyone in the family can do. But I do not want to leave the subject of violent video games just yet.

Brad J. Bushman, social psychologist at The Ohio State University, whose research focuses on the causes and consequences of human aggression, says, "Violent video games might be even more harmful than violent TV programs. While television viewing is usually a passive activity, video game playing is highly interactive. Most violent video games require the player to take on the identity of a violent game character, and most of these games reward individuals for behaving aggressively (for example, players get points for killing people). The violence portrayed in these video games is almost continuous. Scientific research has shown that violent video games increase aggressive thoughts, feelings and behavior. Lamentably, the most popular video games are violent ones."[7]

Anders Behring Breivik, infamous Norwegian mass murderer responsible for the horrific Utøya massacre and Oslo bombing on July 22, 2011, admitted to playing *World of Warcraft* and *Modern Warfare 2* to prepare him for the task of slaughtering.[8] I understand that not everyone who plays *World of Warcraft* uses it to commit heinous crimes, but there is a reason Breivik chose that game and not *Super Mario Galaxy*.

According to Craig Anderson, the director of the Iowa State University Center for the Study of Violence, extreme violence is not expected to occur in normal, well-adjusted individuals simply as a result of playing violent video games. Extreme acts of violence "almost always occur when there is a convergence of multiple risk factors."[9] According to a US surgeon general report in 2001, those risk factors include, "gang involvement, antisocial parents and peers, substance abuse, poverty and media violence." Being male increases this risk.

To quote Ohio State University's Brad Bushman again, in an interview with NPR News, "Playing violent video games probably will not turn your child into a psychopathic killer, but I would want to know how the child treats his or her parents, how they treat their siblings, how much compassion they have."[10]

Another researcher, Professor Ryuta Kawashima at Tohoku University in Japan, found that the tendency to have aggressive meltdowns as a result of playing video games is perhaps not entirely due to children absorbing the aggression involved in the computer game itself, but also due to the damage done by stunting the developing mind. The reason young children have trouble controlling their emotions is that their brains, particularly the frontal lobe, are undeveloped. As they interact with friends, make choices, and are engaged in learning activities, the brains develop and eventually, as they get older, they gain control of their emotions and reactions.[11]

Dr. Kawashima and his team found, using brain scans done while children played video games, that video games only stimulate activity in the parts of the brain that have to do with vision and movement. In contrast, brain scans done while children were engaged in a simple, repetitive, arithmetical exercise "stimulated brain activity in both the left and right hemispheres of the frontal lobe—the area of the brain most associated with learning, memory and emotion."[12] The frontal lobe also plays a key role in controlling behavior, and it continues to develop until age twenty.

Most compellingly, when Dr. Kawashima began his research, he expected to be able to find the hidden benefits associated with video games. Instead he found the opposite— that few video games on the market can claim to be of any benefit to a developing brain. "Children need to be encouraged to learn basic reading and writing," Dr. Kawashima said at a conference in the United Kingdom. "But the other thing is to ask them to play outside with other children and interact and to communicate with others as much as possible. This is how they will develop, retain their creativity and become good people."[13]

So, what is a parent to do? Many of us will find that avoiding video games altogether is tricky if not impossible, maybe not even desirable (included here: computer games, online games, handheld devices, and so on). But setting limits on time and content is crucial, and certainly doable.

In my family, the issue of what types of games are allowed has not been a huge problem yet. Our kids were so thrilled we had a Wii at all that pretty much any game was a delight for them. Still, I confess (as the girl and peace-lover that I am) that even *LEGO Star Wars* contains too much shooting and enemy-defeating for my taste, and we have steered away from these games in favor of the side-scrolling *New Super Mario Bros. Wii* (that holds a little nostalgia for me) and others with more cartoon-like violence.

Solutions for time management can include having certain days of the week or month as "video game days." I know families that do that, and I like this approach. In our case, we noticed that the video game time became a direct competitor with reading for pleasure. So in our family we use a weekly chart to log hours spent reading. For every hour our children spend reading any given week they earn half an hour of Wii time the following week, with a maximum of four hours of Wii per week (still this seems a lot to me!). It has worked well so far and has been mostly a win-win, though the hardest part is for the child to actually turn off the game when the time is up. For this reason we set an alarm to go off when five minutes are left, but often a parent must still be present to either nag and remind or, in some cases, physically press the button.

To end on a positive note, NPR News has also reported that board game sales are up, citing the weaker economy as one contributor to this trend. Families look for more affordable entertainment options in times like these. The report also claims that "the community aspect of face-to-face gaming is what will keep people buying and playing board games even when the economy improves."[14]

And I am happy to report that in our house, board games usually win over video games. So, let's not despair. There is hope for the rising generation and humanity after all.

Notes

1. Donna St. George, "Study Links Violent Video Games, Hostility," *Washington Post*, November 3, 2008, http://www .civicsurvey.org/Study%20Links%20Violent%20Video%20 Games,%20Hostility.pdf.

2. Eyder Peralta, "The Video Game 'Call of Duty' Sets Sales Record," National Public Radio, November 11, 2011, http:// www.npr.org/blogs/thetwo-way/2011/11/11/142257157/the -video-game-call-of-duty-sets-sales-record.

3. Ibid.

4. "Resolution on Violence in Video Games and Interactive Media," American Psychological Association, accessed January 04, 2012, http://www.apa.org/about/governance/council/policy /interactive-media.pdf.

5. *Report of the APA Task Force on the Sexualization of Girls*, American Psychological Association, 2007, http://www.apa.org /pi/women/programs/girls/report.aspx.

6. Craig A. Anderson and Brad J. Bushman, "Effects of Violent Video Games on Aggressive Behavior, Aggressive Cognition, Aggressive Affect, Physiological Arousal, and Prosocial Behavior: A Meta-Analytic Review of the Scientific Literature," *Psychological Science* 12, no. 5 (September 2001): 353–59.

7. Brad J. Bushman, "It's 'Only' Violence," *Ensign*, June 2003, http://lds.org/ensign/2003/06/its-only-violence?lang=eng.

8. "Norway Shooting: Quotes from Anders Behring Breivik's Online Manifesto," Telegraph.co.uk, August 19, 2011, http:// www.telegraph.co.uk/news/worldnews/europe/norway/8657727

/Norway-shooting-quotes-from-Anders-Behring-Breiviks
-online-manifesto.html.

9. Donna St. George, "Study Links Violent Video Games, Hostility," *Washington Post*, November 3, 2008, http://www .civicsurvey.org/Study%20Links%20Violent%20Video%20 Games,%20Hostility.pdf.

10. Shankar Vedantam, "It's a Duel: How Do Violent Video Games Affect Kids?," National Public Radio, July 7, 2011, http://www.npr.org/2011/07/07/137660609/its-a-duel-how-do -violent-video-games-affect-kids.

11. Naomi Coleman, "Are Computer Games Damaging Your Child's Health?," *Daily Mail*, accessed December 23, 2011, http://www.dailymail.co.uk/health/article-67490/Are-games -damaging-childs-health.html.

12. Tracy McVeigh, "Computer Games Stunt Teen Brains," *The Guardian*, August 18, 2001, http://www.guardian.co.uk /world/2001/aug/19/games.schools.

13. Brian Crecente, "Brain Age Professor Attacked Games in 2001," Kotaku, March 31, 2006, http://kotaku.com/164292/brain-age -professor-attacked-games-in-2001.

14. Cheri Lawson, "No Batteries Required: Board Game Sales Soar," National Public Radio, December 24, 2009, http://www .npr.org/templates/story/story.php?storyId=121841016.

NUTRITION

"You cannot achieve environmental security and human development without addressing the basic issues of health and nutrition."

Gro Harlem Brundtland
former Prime Minister of Norway and
Director General of the World Health Organization

FEEDING KIDS SHOULD NOT BE ROCKET SCIENCE, YET I have fussed over this aspect of parenting more than I ever imagined I would. The foods I'd like them to eat versus the ones they prefer ranks high on the list of concerns. I love, love, love my adopted country. I loved it from the first moment I touched new world soil on a hot August day in Chicago. But I trust I will not offend any American who reads this when I say that the food culture in general here leaves something to be desired. It is not completely without merit that Europeans equate America with fast food and obesity. This is, of course, a gross overgeneralization but something Europeans are guilty of nevertheless.

I suppose we all compare our own childhood to that of children today in one way or another, and I know that when I compare the Scandinavia of my childhood to the America of the twenty-first century, it is not fair in the least, because today's Scandinavian children have a much different experience than I did—the same generational type of change that has occurred in the United States.

Our bodies require the same basic nutrition they did thirty or one hundred years ago, and even if we have become more globalized as a society—eating more foods from all over the world—it should not mean that our dietary habits deteriorate to eating so many unhealthy foods that we become sick as a people. Especially when we have a great understanding of what is good and bad for our bodies. But that is nevertheless what it happening today.

It is not difficult to find reliable sources for what a balanced diet should look like. The American Heart Association (AHA), for example, says, "The general dietary recommendations of the AHA for those aged 2 years and older stress a diet that primarily relies on fruits and vegetables, whole grains, low-fat and nonfat dairy products, beans, fish, and lean meat."[1] The National Library of Medicine has published the following handy six points:

- Offer five servings of fruits and vegetables a day
- Choose healthy sources of protein, such as lean meat, nuts, and eggs
- Serve whole-grain breads and cereals because they are high in fiber
- Broil, grill or steam foods instead of frying them
- Limit fast food and junk food
- Offer water and milk instead of sugary fruit drinks and sodas[2]

School children learn these principles as well—meaning they are taught in classrooms, assemblies, and special nutrition-themed weeks. But the story is told differently when we see practices applied. Snacks and school lunches do not exactly comply with the six points above, and many homes are similarly deficient.

So why don't more people follow dietary recommendations? Part of the challenge is the onslaught of junk food–related advertising. We as adults get our fair share of it if we sit down for any length of time in front of the television, and despite what some people may think, advertising does work. It lodges itself in our subliminal mind. And it works especially well on children. Since they have little discernment between information and propaganda, they are extremely susceptible to advertising. And marketers know it.

One study documenting food advertising and marketing toward children concluded that "marketers are intensifying their efforts to develop brand relationships with young consumers, beginning when they are toddlers." The reason marketers are interested in young consumers is "because of their spending power, their purchasing influence, and as future adult consumers. Multiple techniques and channels are used to reach youth, beginning when they are toddlers, to foster brand-building and influence food product purchase behavior. These food marketing channels include television advertising, in-school marketing, product placements, kids clubs, the Internet, toys and products with brand logos, and youth-targeted promotions, such as cross-selling and tie-ins."[3]

The Kaiser Family Foundation reported on results from forty separate studies done on TV ads for children, making it the largest study ever done. The researchers found (not surprisingly) that "exposure to food advertising [does] affect children's food choices and requests for products in the supermarket." The report goes on to say that "the typical child sees about 40,000 ads a year on TV, and that the majority of ads targeted to kids are for candy, cereal, soda and fast food. Furthermore, many of the advertising and marketing campaigns enlist children's favorite TV and movie characters: from SpongeBob Cheez-Its to Scooby-Doo cereals and Teletubbies Happy Meals."[4]

The Institute of Medicine (IOM), in its consensus report *Food Marketing to Children: Threat or Opportunity*, claimed that "Dietary patterns begin in childhood and shape the health of Americans." The IOM concluded that marketing practices are out of balance with recommended diets and that the "current food and beverage marketing practices puts children's long-term health at risk."[5]

The number of overweight children has increased—a phenomenon seen in most of the Western world. But the United States is leading the pack worldwide. In 2009–10, more than 78 million (35.7 percent) US adults and almost 13 million (17 percent) children and adolescents aged two to nineteen were obese. More women than men are reported as obese, but among children more boys are obese than girls. The US obesity rates do not show any evidence of going down.[6] The Center for Disease Control and Prevention (CDC) has stated that since 1980 the percentage of overweight children ages six to eleven has more than doubled, and the rate for adolescents has tripled.[7] It seems this problem could stand being attacked from all angles—at home, at school, and on a policy-making level.

And the issue of child nutrition has been up for political debate recently. Congress has called on the USDA to modify the current standards on food served in schools. The current standards do not specify anything with regard to minimum or maximum levels of fiber, sodium, and sugar. Nor is freely available water a current standard. The proposed changes include that children should consume less than a teaspoon of sodium per day, that 50 percent of all grains be whole grains, and that any food should contain a maximum of 35 percent sugar, based on its weight. Water should be freely available to all children.[8]

But then, in November 2011, Congress passed its now-infamous "pizza is a vegetable" legislation against efforts of the Obama administration to make school lunches healthier. This means that, for now, french fries and pizza will remain approved lunch foods in American schools. Standards proposed by the Department of Agriculture earlier in 2011, which included limits on potatoes and sodium while aiming to boost whole grains, were thus defeated. The bill also famously allows tomato paste on pizzas to be counted as a vegetable, despite the USDA's desire to prevent it.[9]

In the weeks following the passing of this legislation, speculation ensued in the news media. Some argued that the reasons the more stringent requirements for healthy foods were not passed include pressure from food companies whose sales would have been negatively impacted by the proposed changes, and politicians in Congress who don't think the federal government should be telling children what to eat. In my opinion, allowing unhealthy foods into our schools is dictating what they eat just as much as banning them would, so I cannot see this as a solid argument.

Another reason for pushing back against healthier school lunches is said to be that the new regulations would be burdensome and costly for school districts already facing cuts in the budget. I take issue with that argument as well (having been a vegetarian for eight years before I had children and knowing full well that eating nutritious food does not have to be expensive). And so does television chef Jamie Oliver from the United Kingdom (also known as "The Naked Chef" because of his love for "naked"—not processed—ingredients). He has been outspoken about the need for school lunch reform in his native country as well as in the United States. "I've spent time in Italy and seen the poorest of people eating the most delicious—but really inexpensive—food because they know how to use ingredients," says Jamie Oliver. "I've been to South Africa and seen women in shantytowns preparing meals for school kids that cost a few cents but had huge nutritional value."[10]

He also points out that the food we eat affects school children in so many ways, including "mood, behavior, health, growth, even [their] ability to concentrate. A lunchtime school meal should provide a growing child with one-third their daily nutritional intake."[11] Considering the education crisis we are facing as a nation, it is not unreasonable to me that we should improve nutrition. Students would concentrate better, and teachers would be faced with a more balanced crowd in their classrooms if we did. Parents can attest to the difference it makes when a child has had oatmeal and eggs for breakfast as opposed to waffles and sausage drenched in syrup. May I add that the latter is more expensive?

And according to news reports, our own government recently bought seven million pounds of ammonia-treated meat to use for school lunches.[12] You may have heard of "pink slime"—the pictures of which got people so outraged on Facebook and the Internet in general that McDonald's, Taco Bell, and Burger King finally decided to stop using it.[13] The product consists of a combination of beef scraps, cow connective tissues, and other beef trimmings instead of muscle. It is then ground and blended and treated with ammonium hydroxide to kill salmonella and E. coli and other pathogens. The nutritional value does not equal that of real muscle meat. But it is apparently good enough for school kids, according to the government.

To avoid the junk food served in the school cafeteria and to save money, I try to pack our children's school lunches daily. Like everything else, it is ultimately up to parents to ensure their children's well-being. But there are many parents out there who cannot or at least do not see to the basic necessity of a balanced diet.

I will never forget how some of my teacher friends, who work in some of the poorest schools in Oklahoma City, described the positive impact that an initiative of serving an afternoon snack had on the children. The snacks consisted of fruits and vegetables, and, according to the teachers, at the outset of this initiative, some of the children had never eaten an apple before.

Children are affected not only on a daily basis by what they eat; it has long-term outcomes as well. We know that children who are overweight run a higher risk of becoming adults who are obese. Health professionals often point out that American children consume far too much sugar and salt.

Reading from a box of glazed, shredded wheat type cereal, my son asked one morning, "Mom, did you know that the recommended daily intake of fiber is twenty-five to thirty-five grams but that less than half of all Americans eat that much?"

"Yes, son, I think I knew that," I replied, grateful that he was beginning to take his seat among the enlightened ones.

But when he tried to convince me that the same cereal is healthy because of its six grams of fiber, I automatically pointed to the eleven grams of sugar, because that is the kind of kill-joy mother I am when it comes to junk food.

"But it's only eleven grams," he said. "I have seen foods with thirty-five grams of sugar, so this is less than a third of that."

"Yes, my dear, but there is no daily nutritional minimum intake for refined sugar. None. Zip. Zilch. The body does not need it at all."

The world of sugar is a tricky one. Sugar is in everything

processed, it seems, even ketchup. And if there is no sugar, there's often bound to be some kind of corn syrup. Parents sometimes believe that avoiding the much-debated high fructose corn syrup in favor of pure fruit juices is doing their children a favor. Though fruit juice is no doubt a better choice than beverages made from high fructose corn syrup, parents should think twice about letting their child drink too freely from fruit juices. Excessive fruit juice consumption has been documented to be associated with obesity and short stature, even after adjustments were made for parental stature. "Excessive consumption" in one study was determined as more than twelve ounces per day. An approximately three centimeter difference was documented in two-year-olds, between excessive and nonexcessive juice drinkers, and a five centimeter difference was seen in five-year-olds.[14]

More and more children are being diagnosed with type 2 diabetes, an illness usually seen in adults over forty. Major contributors to the increase of this disease among children and adolescents are the epidemics of obesity and the sedentary lifestyles of today's young people.[15] The CDC states, "Children and adolescents diagnosed with type 2 diabetes are generally between 10 and 19 years old, obese, have a strong family history for type 2 diabetes, and have insulin resistance."[16]

Sodium, another dietary culprit if consumed in excess, can be found in rather elevated levels in many processed foods. According to the Institute of Medicine in a 2010 report, the American sodium intake far exceeds the recommended amounts, which increases the risk for high blood pressure, "a serious health condition that is avoidable and can lead to a variety of diseases."[17] The same report also claims that if we would reduce our sodium intake, it could prevent more than 100,000 deaths per year. "Without major change," says the report, "hypertension and cardio-vascular disease rates will continue to rise."[18] Think you're not one of them? Nine out of ten Americans consume too much sodium.[19] A good portion of it is said to come from pizza, cookies, and meats.

One way to help our children avoid excessive sodium is to help shape their taste preferences early in life by not feeding them any salt the first year and giving them very sparing amounts after, avoiding those foods with high sodium content. At least one study has found that early dietary experiences help shape the "salty taste responses of infants and young children," suggesting that we do not have to feel completely helpless as parents when it comes to guiding their diet.[20] But as with everything else in parenting, it does require a little bit of effort.

When I had only one child, this was more doable. It was easier to cook saltless foods (for the purpose of also going easy on the developing kidneys) when I had fewer people to cook for and less responsibility on the whole. And I confess that child three and child four have not gotten quite the same conscientious treatment at the dinner table. I do worry about our youngest, Julia, from time to time. She always wants salt on her food when she sees anyone salting theirs, and we oblige by passing the salt shaker over her food without actually releasing any salt. Thank goodness for the placebo effect.

Cooking for a family is not always the joy I wish it were. When I go to prepare dinner I automatically envision how many of the kids will object at such and such dish if I make it, and if it was the same child who objected to yesterday's dinner, then it does influence my choice of menu. I have collected a few dishes that everyone in our family likes, the nutrition content of which I am reasonably happy about. I cook these dishes more often than I would if I were feeding only my husband and myself, simply for the sake of peace at the dinner table and to be sure everyone gets a decent meal.

And there are so many factors that go into getting kids to eat. Elina, when she was young, was the skinniest little thing you ever saw, and having a very small appetite, she seemed to only eat a substantial meal a few times a week. She also had a sensitive gag reflex. Among the times she actually did eat a hearty meal, far too many ended with her choking on the last bite and—forgive the graphic—all her dinner came up along with some of her lunch. How often I despaired over this! But in spite of it, she has grown very tall, and today she is the healthiest eater in the family, still with a modest appetite (what I would not give to have that natural portion control). She loves salads, lentil and bean dishes, crunchy whole grain unsweetened foods, and vegetable stews and soups, so my worries about her have completely ceased in this department and I can turn my attention to the junk-food-lovers in the house.

I try to remember that things can and do change for the better if we do not give up, but it usually takes time, and changes are gradual. This helps me to fret less over the cries in our house for food that in my mind does not meet the definition of food. I also have more patience with Julia's refusal to drink milk and find myself navigating the world of alternative calcium sources with a more positive attitude.

Notes

1. "AHA Scientific Statement Dietary Recommendations for Children and Adolescents. A Guide for Practitioners: Consensus Statement From the American Heart Association," American Heart Association 112 (2005): 2061–75, doi:10.1161/.
2. "Child Nutrition," Medline Plus, accessed January 3, 2012, http://www.nlm.nih.gov/medlineplus/childnutrition.html.
3. Mary Story and Simone French, "Food Advertising and Marketing Directed at Children and Adolescents in the US,"

The International Journal of Behavioral Nutrition and Physical Activity 1, no. 3 (February 10, 2004), doi:10.1186/1479-5868-1-3.

4. The Henry J. Kaiser Family Foundation, "Kaiser Family Foundation Releases a New Report on the Role of Media in Childhood Obesity," news release, accessed January 3, 2012, http://www.kff.org/entmedia/entmedia022404nr.cfm.

5. "Food Marketing to Children and Youth: Threat or Opportunity?," Institute of Medicine, accessed December 5, 2005, http://www.iom.edu/Reports/2005/Food-Marketing-to -Children-and-Youth-Threat-or-Opportunity.aspx.

6. Cynthia L. Ogden, Margaret D. Carroll, Brian K. Kit, and Katherine M. Flegal, "Prevalence of Obesity in the United States, 2009–2010," Centers for Disease Control and Prevention, January 2012, http://www.cdc.gov/nchs/data/databriefs/db82 .pdf.

7. The Henry J. Kaiser Family Foundation, "Kaiser Family Foundation Releases a New Report on the Role of Media in Childhood Obesity," news release, accessed January 3, 2012, http://www.kff.org/entmedia/entmedia022404nr.cfm.

8. "The Basics about School Lunch: A Brief Overview," Jamie Oliver's Food Revolution, accessed January 3, 2012, http://www .jamieoliver.com/us/foundation/jamies-food-revolution/__cms /uploads/4_Support%20Tool_The%20Basics.pdf.

9. Mary Clare Jalonick, "Pizza is a vegetable? Congress says yes," MSNBC.com, November 15, 2011, http://www.msnbc .msn.com/id/45306416/ns/health-diet_and_nutrition/t/pizza -vegetable-congress-says-yes/.

10. Lauren P. Kennedy, "Chef Jamie Oliver Makes Over School Lunches," WebMD, August 8, 2008, http://www.webmd.com /diet/features/chef_jamie_oliver_makes_over_school_lunches ?page=2.

11. Ibid.

12. Emmeline Zhao, "Pink Slime for School Lunch: Government Buying 7 Million Pounds of Ammonia-Treated Meat for Meals," *Huffington Post*, March 05, 2012, http://www.huffington post.com/2012/03/05/pink-slime-for-school-lun_n_1322325 .html?ncid=edlinkusaolp00000009.

13. M. Alex Johnson, "McDonald's Drops Use of Gooey Ammonia-based 'Pink Slime' in Hamburger Meat," *U.S. News*,

January 31, 2012, http://usnews.msnbc.msn.com/_news/2012/01/31/10282876-mcdonalds-drops-use-of-gooey-ammonia-based-pink-slime-in-hamburger-meat; Emmeline Zhao, "Pink Slime for School Lunch: Government Buying 7 Million Pounds of Ammonia-Treated Meat for Meals." *Huffington Post*, March 5, 2012, http://www.huffingtonpost.com/2012/03/05/pink-slime-for-school-lun_n_1322325.html?ncid=edlinkusaolp00000009.

14. Barbara A. Dennison, Helen L. Rockwell, and Sharon L. Baker, "Excess Fruit Juice Consumption by Preschool-aged Children Is Associated with Short Stature and Obesity," *Pediatrics* 99, no. 1 (January 1, 1997): 15–22.

15. "Children and Diabetes," Centers for Disease Control and Prevention, May 20, 2011, http://www.cdc.gov/diabetes/projects/cda2.htm.

16. Ibid.

17. Institute of Medicine, "Strategies to Reduce Sodium Intake in the United States," report, April 20, 2010, http://iom.edu/Reports/2010/Strategies-to-Reduce-Sodium-Intake-in-the-United-States.aspx.

18. Ibid.

19. "90% of Americans Get Too Much Sodium," LiveScience.com, June 24, 2010, http://www.livescience.com/8362-90-americans-sodium.html.

20. Leslie J. Stein, Beverly J. Cowart, and Gary K. Beauchamp, "The Development of Salty Taste Acceptance Is Related to Dietary Experience in Human Infants: A Prospective Study," *American Journal of Clinical Nutrition* 95, no. 1 (January 2012): 123–29, doi:10.3945/.

MONEY

"Annual income twenty pounds, annual expenditure nineteen six, result happiness. Annual income twenty pounds, annual expenditure twenty pounds ought and six, result misery."

David Copperfield by Charles Dickens

IN THESE UNCERTAIN ECONOMIC TIMES, WATCHING GOV-ernments and companies fail because of poor money management and then pass the cost on to . . . well, me . . . I wonder if these political and business leaders were ever taught about money in a real way at home (or perhaps the question should be: "Were they taught anything about honesty and ethics?").

Whatever the cause for our dismal leadership in money management, statistics show a bleak picture of American children's and teens' financial literacy skills. Out of the four thousand students who took the Jump$tart personal finance survey, a whopping 65.5 percent received failing scores. And yet, a study conducted in 2005 found that 21 percent of eighteen- and nineteen-year-olds had credit cards.[1]

Thankfully, some improvements have been made in this area since then. The Credit CARD Act of 2009 made it illegal for people under age twenty-one to get credit cards unless they can show proof of income or they have a cosigner over the age of twenty-one.[2]

In 2008, only 59 percent of the young adults in Generation Y (ages eighteen to twenty-one) paid their bills on time every month. The same research also found that almost 50 percent of those who closely monitor their finances say that they learned about personal finance from their parents or at home more frequently than those who had more lax money-management practices.[3]

I remember well the day I sat in a marriage-prep class when I was twenty-two and the teacher announced that the next week's lesson would be on the number one cause for divorce. Everyone in the class perked up. What could that be?

"Money!"

Okay, so not just money—but the disagreement over how money should be spent, the mismanagement of money, the lack of money, handling debt, and the stress of money. Statistics show that couples who report arguing about finances once a week are over 30 percent more likely to get divorced than those who report disagreeing about finances a few times a month.[4]

Although people spend hours planning their wedding, they often spend little time discussing how they will handle their financial resources together. Imagine a world where, before getting married, couples talked about their values, how they would like to use their money together, their feelings about debt, and how they will make financial decisions together. Investment of time and effort before the wedding would likely mitigate some of the confusion, misunderstanding, and arguments about money that often ensue in most marriages. I'd like to think that the lack of money would be a factor in adding financial stress to married couples. And, as the economy goes down, divorce goes up, though even large amounts of money can be mismanaged and cause unhappiness. Research shows, "Thrifty couples are the happiest!"[5] Happiness through thriftiness can only happen if couples agree together (ideally before they get married) to save, spend less, and not be driven by material acquisition.

The statistics go on and on and speak one clear message to me as a parent: "Teach your kids how to manage money!" Children will use money long before they ever really earn it. Their (and perhaps their children's) happiness, health, and success in life depends on their ability to manage money.

But when we teach about money, we ought to remember that money is often just the expression of desire. Perhaps the real beast to tame is the force that drives expenditures—the choices we make and why we make them. How strong is that beast? Well, let's consider the never-ending onslaught of marketing directed at today's kids. Campaign for a Commercial-Free Childhood gathered some rather startling numbers in 2008 concerning marketing to children. According to the campaign, "companies spend about $17 billion annually marketing to children, a staggering increase from the $100 million spent in 1983. Children under 14 spend about $40 billion annually. Compare this to the $6.1 billion 4–12 year olds spent in 1989. Teens spend about $159 billion. Children under 12 influence $500 billion in purchases per year. This generation of children is the most brand-conscious ever. Teens between 13 and 17 have 145 conversations about brands per week, about twice as many as adults."[6]

If that doesn't make us want to rope in commercial influences in our children's lives, perhaps this will at least make us think twice about our living room habits: "Children ages 2–11 see more than 25,000 advertisements a year on TV alone."[7]

One time when I was at Walmart with all four kids in tow, an older man halted as he met us in the aisle. He looked carefully at each of the children and then at me.

"Well," he said, "I see that you brought a whole team of financial advisors with you today."

I laughed. How right he was!

Who hasn't been through the store, having the kids help find items on the list only to be bombarded with demands like, "Mom, can we buy these fruit snacks?"

"No, honey, they are expensive and filled with high fructose corn syrup."

"But they're only five dollars. That's not very much."

"Actually, it is a lot when you consider what you get."

A friend of mine, a mother of two, always poured her cold cereal into clear plastic containers as soon as she came home from grocery shopping. I complimented her on the containers when I stayed overnight at her house with my then-only child, and she explained to me that it was not for their looks that she had gotten them, but because she was trying to reduce the marketing aimed at her small children. It seemed rather a chore to me to go through this extra step then, but I can sympathize with her efforts now.

Even more pervasive than commercial packaging is the effect of television. Limiting or eliminating exposure to commercial television will probably do more than all other strategies combined (except parental example, of course) to quash children's desire to consume. A friend of mine does not allow her two children to watch television in their home. Before the holidays every year, they have a tradition of writing letters to Santa Claus. For three years in a row, her daughter asked Santa to bring "whatever he felt was best." This year, at age eight, she clipped out one item totaling fifteen dollars from the Scholastic book order form (that she received in school, no less) and taped it to her letter to

Santa. Her mother is certain limited exposure to television in particular "keeps the beast" of materialistic desires in check in her children.

It is fair to assume, based on this aggressive marketing to children and our letting our kids be marketed to through our own choices (our allowance of television consumption and our own striving to "keep up with the Joneses"), that their wants will far exceed their means. It seems that this will always remain a great challenge to engender any sort of balanced understanding of real value and cost in their early years. While limiting television, Internet, and other media exposure may be inconvenient to us in the short term, it may have a big long-term impact on our children's ability to defer gratification and manage money.

Equally important is the example we provide. If our children hear us comparing our standard of living to that of other families and see us buying what is "new and shiny" and purchasing far beyond what we need, our words are hollow for our children when it comes to money management. The patterns of desire, spending, saving, and handling economic choices are set in childhood, and what children see has a greater impact than what they hear. This is especially true if what they see contradicts what we tell them concerning how money is handled.

And if children are unlucky, they will be showered with gifts for birthdays, Christmas, and other occasions that are not only expensive but also many in number, adding to the potential for developing a skewed sense of materialistic standard that they might expect to maintain.

We are in difficult economic times as a nation, yet there is no evidence that marketing toward children is slowing down, despite the fact that many parents have less buying power. But hopefully many children will witness monetary restraint by their parents these days. Is the silver lining of our recession that more children will grow up with a greater appreciation for what they have?

A friend of my son (then in pre-K), whose parents were living on the meager financial diet that full-time PhD studies often bring, had his mother nearly in tears when he came home from school and announced that his teacher required him to have a larger backpack (his current one being much too small to accommodate his schoolbooks and papers).

Hoping to preserve a modicum of pride and not have to divulge the honest truth—that they truly could not afford a new backpack right then—his mom did not immediately turn to friends whose children might have an extra book bag gathering dust in some closet. Instead, she did some research and found out about the National Backpack Program run by Office Depot, which "places new backpacks into the hands of children who might not otherwise have the proper tools for success."[8] Later that day, the little boy sat smiling on the couch, hugging his donated book bag.

"Mom, I just had the best day! I got to go to the city, and I got a brand new backpack," he volunteered.

How many of us parents would not pay money to instill that sort of gratitude in our children's hearts? But to achieve that effect, we might have to of course learn to withhold more money. I believe strongly that a crucial ingredient to lifelong happiness is to experience delayed gratification in childhood—to wish, long for, and work toward things that we cannot have right now and perhaps not for some time.

My parents taught me by powerful example. They were both twenty years old the year I was born, neither of them college educated, yet on a very limited income, they practiced financial responsibility that would have made most personal finance educators proud. My parents prioritized having a nice home where my dad did almost all the work himself—adding pretty but inexpensive finishes and furnishings while my mom sewed the curtains and upholstered the chairs. My dad made himself sandwiches every morning to take to work along with a bottle of juice. He never ate out. The lesson that eating at home saves money was never explicitly taught to me. I knew it by watching my parents.

Our most feared expense: cars! My parents were committed to paying cash. These cars were not usually pretty to look at, nor did they always prove to be dependable long-term. We had a particularly ugly, orange Volvo station wagon with three doors that were different colors (from parts cars) and whose brakes squealed so loudly that our Labrador could hear and recognize the sound when it was two blocks away.

I also recall a yellow Datsun whose driver's side door only opened from the inside and whose lights only worked when on the bright setting. We lived in the deep forest of the Swedish countryside at that time, and in the winter when my mother drove me to the bus stop two and a half miles away before sunrise, she would turn off the brights for coming cars (as is the law) and everything would go black on our side of the road.

I don't remember being particularly grateful for those experiences at the time. Yet, as an adult, they comprise some of my most cherished childhood memories. Perhaps they would be less cherished if the frugal choices my parents made early on had not begun to noticeably pay off and eventually land them in the comfortable situation where they are today.

Parents can take many different approaches to teach their children about money. But one of the most important components of any such education is to allow children the opportunity to use money, to let them spend it unwisely (as most are inclined to do at some point), and not to rescue the child from the consequences. As parents, how can we create such experiences? One way is providing an allowance. The question of allowance is a difficult one fraught with different options.

Inger Giuffrida, financial educator and asset-building consultant (and my personal friend), writes and speaks often to parents about allowance. She emphasizes that allowance can "provide context for teaching children about money. Having an allowance can help children learn about:

- The value of money
- Planning (and saving) for bigger purchases than they can afford at the present
- Using money to reach a goal
- Developing a budget
- Sharing financial resources through charitable giving, and
- Not being able to get everything they want when they want it."[9]

These valuable life lessons stick when they are experienced, and allowance can provide the foundation for those experiences.

She also encourages families to set broad parameters about how the money can be used. This can help determine how much allowance to give. For example, a set of guidelines she recommends includes

- 25 percent of the allowance goes to savings or living independently after high school
- 25 percent goes to charitable contributions, including faith-based contributions, and
- 50 percent can be used however the child wants to use it: discretionary spending. This is where savings for a desire occurs too.

She is commonly asked about tying allowance to chores. She emphasizes that this sends a clear message—you get paid for taking care of your responsibilities. If, however, you want to instill a natural sense of responsibility for contributions around the household, she recommends separating allowance from chores. This means that chores are just daily or weekly expectations. This also means that allowance cannot be withheld if chores are not completed.

I know Inger, and she does not pay allowance for chores. She wants her kids to know that making their beds, picking up their toys, setting the table, and helping clean the house are part of being a member of a family—not activities that deserve remuneration. (She does provide her children additional opportunities for earning money through their contributions to big projects, such as cleaning out the garage or helping paint the house.)

Clearly, judging by the statistics listed earlier, children in our country *do* have the opportunity to spend money. But if the young people (and adults) of today have such poor money management skills, the lessons must be lost somewhere along the way, if they are taught at all.

Children will need to make mistakes such as spending everything at once, impulse buying, and purchasing an overpriced, cheaply made product and simply experience the resulting disappointment and regret without bailout. We would hate to set a precedent that suggests parents will rescue adult credit card debt, right? Experience gained over a few wasted dollars while young may translate into behavior that controls larger amounts of money when older. Allowance can give them the resources to do this. Parents can certainly consult and give advice but would do well to step back and let kids make their own choices when the amounts are relatively small. We can then illuminate less-than-stellar examples of spending for future improvement.

I also argue that earning money by hard work (or saving limited allowance funds over a period of time) increases its value and makes the buyer a more careful spender. I have seen this in my own kids, and I recall it from my own childhood. I saved my allowance for four weeks to buy one My Little Pony, and during those four weeks, I often went to check on the pony in the store to make sure it was still there. Not only was I more careful with my money when I had earned it (or saved my meager allowance for a long time), I was also more careful with the things I bought, remembering their cost and the time involved to afford them.

It is also important to engage children in conversations about family spending so they understand that adults have to make priorities and choices over spending on a daily basis. How will children learn to control their spending if they don't see this restraint practiced? To that end, my husband and I hide very little from our children when it comes to our finances. But I had cause to question the well-roundedness of our home finance curriculum when Elina, seven, took a fall and we suspected a broken arm (indeed, it was). She refused, at first, to be taken to urgent care to have her arm X-rayed.

"It costs too much money!" she cried, well aware that our medical insurance coverage left much to be desired.

I felt a huge pang of motherly guilt and thought that perhaps we had overemphasized money and the need to save it. Clearly, a lesson in needs versus wants was in order, as well as reassurance that our children's health and well-being goes before any monetary consideration.

In the end, money is a tool. But just as with all tools, learning how to use it properly takes instruction. We can provide that through direct teaching and by example. And we must do this, because if children don't learn about money management and fiscal responsibility from their parents, who is going to teach them? The government. Their peers. The marketers and advertisers.

Notes

1. "Financial Literacy Statistics," Washington State Department of Financial Institutions, January 29, 2010, http://www.dfi .wa.gov/consumers/financial_literacy_stats.htm.

2. Alinda J. Murphy and Inger K. Giuffrida, "The Credit CARD Act: A Webinar for Financial Educators," Federal Reserve Bank of Kansas City, March 9, 2010, http://www.kansascityfed.org /publicat/community/Webinar.2010.03.08.pdf.

3. "Financial Literacy Statistics," Financial Educators Council, http://www.financialeducatorscouncil.org/financial-literacy -statistics.html.

4. Catherine Rampell, "Money Fights Predict Divorce Rates," NYTimes.com, December 7, 2009, http://economix.blogs .nytimes.com/2009/12/07/money-fights-predict-divorce-rates/.

5. "The State of Our Unions: Marriage in America 2009," University of Virginia, November 2009, http://www.virginia .edu/marriageproject/pdfs/Union_11_25_09.pdf.

6. "Marketing to Our Children Overview," Campaign for a Commercial-Free Childhood, 2008, http://www.commercial freechildhood.org/factsheets/overview.pdf.

7. Ibid.

8. "National Backpack Program," Office Depot Company Information, 2008, http://www.community.officedepot.com /local.asp.

9. Inger Giuffrida, interview by author, January 11, 2012; Inger K. Giuffrida, "Allowance: To Give or Not to Give," *The Word*, August 2009.

READING

"Today a reader, tomorrow a leader."

Margaret Fuller

AS SO OFTEN IS THE CASE, THE GROUP OF SOCIETY THAT needs to be reached by this information will not be. Instead this becomes a sermon that likely only the choir will hear. Because you are, in fact, reading a book. But do read on, as I think you will find the information interesting, useful, and in some cases downright alarming.

Children in our schools desperately need to improve their reading skills. SAT reading scores for graduating high-school seniors reached the lowest point in nearly forty years in 2011.[1] Tests have been rightfully criticized for measuring only a portion of students' abilities, and other factors may affect these scores (such as increased numbers of students whose first language is not English), but regardless of our view of testing as a measuring tool or the incompleteness of the picture this statistic represents, I think we can all agree that the trend is worrisome.

I did my own qualitative research on the decline in reading, rather unintentionally, in my home country. Sweden has long been known as one of the "readingest" countries in the world. In 2006 I spent seven weeks back home with my then-two- and four-year-old children. As we rode buses and trains, I was always pleased to look around and see everyone (from the kid with a Mohawk, tattoo on his neck, and metal-studded leather jacket to the middle-aged executive and the little old lady in the beige trench coat) immersed in a novel. I made note of it again and again during those seven weeks and realized that I had witnessed this all the time growing up but failed to really notice because the sight was so common. Having been separated from this view for some time, living in America, I noticed it more when I returned home.

At my mother's and my combined birthday party I listened to my mom and my uncle (a former special-ed student who never graduated from high school) discuss the latest series of tomes they had both read, comparing and contrasting it to other books and series, naming authors I had only heard of.

In Sweden, reading has long been for everyone, almost regardless of a person's level of education. To feed this desire for reading, a huge book sale is held every February. Every store that carries books will set up huge bargain tables with piles and piles of books. People line up at midnight to be the first to get their hands on special editions and limited-availability books.

I have been fortunate to go back to Sweden nearly every year since I moved to the United States, and gradually the reading scenery has changed—at least in public places. Finally, in May of 2011, I noticed a remarkable difference from my stay in 2006. This time, people were far less likely to be caught reading books at the train station, at the bus stops, or while riding public transportation. And not because they were holding a Kindle or a Nook. Instead, they were obsessively texting, checking Facebook, or playing games on their iPhones and other smartphones. Cell phones are nothing new to Sweden, and it has long been one of the most cell phone dense countries in the world, but it is the advent of the smartphone that seems to finally have pushed the novel out of people's hands. Though mine was not a hard study, I know these observations do not entirely lack merit.

Even our own president, Barack Obama, who has confessed to be addicted to his BlackBerry, has lamented the "24/7 media environment that bombards us with all kinds of content and exposes us to all kinds of arguments, some of which don't always rank all that high on the truth meter. With iPods and iPads . . . information becomes a distraction, a diversion, a form of entertainment, rather than a tool of empowerment."[2] Fewer and fewer people sit down and focus for any length of time on one piece of reading material, such as a book. Instead we skip via hyperlinks to the next thing that catches our eye.

My own elementary school children, who often ride the school bus in the afternoon, are quick to point out that over half the kids have iPhones or iPads that they play with while riding home. I hope that their estimate at 50 percent is an exaggeration for my "benefit" to illustrate the "oppressive nature" of our family, which doesn't even have a portable DVD player for car trips.

"Doesn't anyone read a book while waiting for or riding the bus?" I ask.

"A few. But not very many," comes the reply.

And I know that my children are not likely among those few. Instead I am confident that they are leaning over the seat in front of them to watch the screen of the handheld device in the hand of some third grader.

Our brains do not go unaffected by this. It is almost frightening how quickly and extensively Internet use reroutes people's neural pathways. In only five hours spent online, a novice Internet user can rewire his or her brain, a study shows. And it is not necessarily for the better.[3] Our attention span suffers, as does our learning.

A study by the Broadcaster Audience Research Board found teenagers now spend seven and a half hours a day in front of a screen.[4] Since there are only twenty-four hours in a day and so many things to do, how do they manage this? Seven and a half hours is almost an entire workday. Some of this time may be in school, engaged in legitimate educational pursuits. But what about the rest of the time? I presume many of these teens have their own smartphones, laptops, and TVs in their rooms. How else can they manage it? Where yesterday's teens had their noses in a book at the bus stop and during the ride to school, today's teens are tweeting, texting, Facebooking, and playing games during their spare minutes. This must be the answer, at least in part, to why reading abilities among American teens have suffered so dramatically in recent years.

What can we do then, as parents, to help our children become better readers in the face of all the distractions that surround us?

The Organization for Economic Cooperation and Development (OECD) conducts exams every three years as part of the Program for International Student Assessment (PISA). These tests examine the world's leading industrialized nations' fifteen-year-olds on their reading comprehension, among other things. Needless to say, American fifteen-year-olds have not been among the most impressive. In 2009, PISA did an in-depth study that was conducted over five thousand parents to see what at-home factors influence students for good or bad.[5] The conclusion is not all that surprising. "Fifteen-year-old students whose parents often read books with them during their first year of primary school show markedly higher scores in PISA 2009 than students whose parents read with them infrequently or not at all." And the good news is that "the performance advantage among students whose parents read to them in their early school years is evident regardless of the family's socio-economic background."[6]

The benefits of parents reading to their children is not at all new knowledge, but the following is truly compelling: "On average, the score difference [between parents who read to their children in their early school years and those who did not] is 25 points, which is the equivalent of well over *half a school year*."[7]

The study goes on to report that, "PISA findings also show that other parent-child activities, such as 'discussing books, films or television programmes,' 'discussing how well children are doing at school,' 'eating main meals together around the table' and 'spending time just talking with one's children' are also associated with better student reading performance in school."[8]

According to a *New York Times* report, Andreas Schleicher, who oversees the exams for the OECD, claims that "just asking your child how was their school day and showing genuine interest in the learning that they are doing can have the same impact as hours of private tutoring."[9] Also, it has been noted that dads who read provide a powerful and lasting example to their sons.

The National School Boards Association's (NSBA) Center for Public Education (CPE) reported similar results on their own study ("Back to School: How parent involvement affects student achievement") in the *American School Board Journal*. "Parent involvement can take many forms, but only a few of them relate to higher student performance," the report states. "Of those that work, parental actions that support children's learning at home are most likely to have an impact on academic achievement at school." Some of these actions include "monitoring homework, making sure their kids get to school, rewarding their efforts, and talking up going to college."[10]

As a mother, I have always been daunted by this need to sit down and read with the children and fully expose them to this wonderful world. With four kids, something is always going on, and bedtime can sometimes be madness. Though I am happy to report that we read with the kids every night, with rare exceptions, I also confess that we don't read as much as I would like, and I am consistently working to improve it. This was especially true when my oldest was five, my second was three, and I had just given birth to my third child. Sitting down to read was often a very short excursion.

It was during that time that I started playing audio books in their room at bedtime, simply because the baby was usually screaming, the dishes were not done, and I was beyond tired. My husband or I still managed to read five or ten minutes to the oldest two during these early months of being parents to three. But once we had read to them, we would augment the experience by turning on an audiobook. And it was very well received. I also started to turn on a story in the mornings, fifteen minutes before it was time to get out of bed, to ease the rude awakening. I even recorded myself reading stories to the kids and created a "listening center" in our house, where they could turn on their favorite stories and follow along with the book. We can listen with delight to those tapes now, hearing their much younger voices making adorable comments about the characters and plot.

I invested in Swedish audiobooks as well (our children are bilingual), and I was amazed that the children's Swedish vocabulary and fluency flourished after they started to listen to them consistently.

If these anecdotes are not enough, let me list more reasons to love audiobooks for kids:

1. Kids can listen on their own, greatly expanding the amount of time immersed in literature in addition to being read to by parents.
2. It enables kids to experience books beyond their reading level that are still within their level of comprehension.
3. Audiobooks model good expressive reading that kids will often mimic when they read on their own, which increases comprehension.
4. We can listen in the car, squeezing in that valuable exposure to books while going places (dare to resist the DVD player!).
5. It provides an entertainment option other than screen time.
6. When children begin to tackle the reading of more difficult books, their having listened to audiobooks will help their comprehension.
7. Research supports that listening to audiobooks improves vocabulary, reading fluency, comprehension, and academic performance.[11]

Audiobooks should not replace printed books or parents reading to their children, of course, but they certainly can play an important part in raising and improving a reader. In our family, we have allowed the kids to earn the privilege of seeing a child-friendly, popular movie based on a children's book by first reading (or listening to) the book. For us, this worked well with the Spiderwick series by Holly Black and Tony DiTerlizzi.

After viewing the movie, comparing and contrasting the book and movie then becomes great fodder for discussion. We learned firsthand one time, however, that reading something in a book (or hearing it on audio) is often not nearly as scary as seeing it on screen. When our then-almost-seven-year-old listened to *Harry Potter and the Sorcerer's Stone* (narrated by the genius Jim Dale) and enthusiastically settled in on the couch for the reward of viewing the film, little did we know that for a month we would have to go before the child and turn the lights on in the bathroom just to make sure Voldemort was not hiding there.

Another type of literature I absolutely love is graphic novels or comic books. Just like with any media, however, parents need to screen the content of a graphic novel before presenting it to their kids. Our son spent many hours in second grade reading and rereading the absolutely brilliant Bone series by Jeff Smith as well as the marvelous Amulet series by Kazu Kibuishi. His mother got hooked too! On Amazon .com, I got a dozen or so used *Calvin and Hobbes* collection books for only a few pennies each, plus shipping. Besides being so funny, these strips are filled with wisdom and integrity that is still extremely relevant, even though Bill Watterson stopped drawing the comic in 1995. In my house, if someone suddenly laughs hysterically in his or her bedroom right around bedtime, it is often because they are clutching a *Calvin and Hobbes* volume. I love having the chore of trying to pry a book out of the kids' hands to get them to turn out the light at night.

Not only do graphic novels hold value in and of themselves as reading material, they can also provide a bridge and a gateway into traditional literature and print.[12] This is especially true for reluctant readers, special needs children, English language learners, and other kids who do not read well. Readers can often make sense of overall meanings and concepts in graphic books even if they do not possess the full vocabulary used. With interest and motivation in engaging titles, however, they will get there eventually.

Stephen Krashen, renowned second-language-acquisition researcher and education authority, citing his own research, claims that "middle school boys who read comic books read more in general than boys who did not read comics, read more books, and enjoyed reading more."[13] Krashen also points out the correlation that students who read more, read better, and those who read better, read more.

The visual clues along with the words help and encourage the reader in comprehension, propelling him or her forward in a story whose written descriptive world the reader might not have understood nor had the patience to get through.[14]

Visual clues in graphic books are not always simple, nor do they necessarily cater to a lazy reader.[15] At times, a careful study of the pictures is required to not miss clues that may be vital to the plot. Just because a student is a beginner or struggling reader does not mean he or she is unintelligent or not up for a challenge. Navigating a clever and intellectually stimulating graphic novel is not the same as struggling to get through pages of text in a chapter book. Most students find the former much more enjoyable and are therefore likely to stick with the task until they succeed.

Much anecdotal evidence by teachers, parents, and students also suggests that reading graphic books does not hinder but rather encourages the reading of traditional print literature. Krashen writes, "Several eminent writers and thinkers give comics the credit for helping them develop the competence for, and interest in, 'heavier' reading. Among them is South Africa's Bishop Desmond Tutu."[16] Tutu, who was not a native English speaker, specifically credits comics for helping him learn English better.

Though I'm no Desmond Tutu, I can to some degree echo this claim. As a child, I grew up speaking Norwegian and Swedish, but I never went to a Norwegian school.

Because the Norwegian dialect my family and I spoke in Narvik, Norway, is significantly different compared to written Bokmål Norwegian, writing was difficult for me. From the time I could read, my grandmother gave me money to buy Donald Duck comics on Mondays when I came for our regular extended visits, and over time my collection grew to fill the nightstand drawers of my room in their house. Every time I visited, I read them over again, and to this day, I have to credit them that I can compose letters in Norwegian with a modicum of accuracy.

Even though the reading ability of American children leaves much to be desired, we as parents can and should take heart that with little (but consistent) effort, our child need not be among those whose ability falls below benchmarks. Indeed, we can hope to instill more than just adequate reading abilities; we can light the flame of a lifelong love for reading.

Notes

1. Michael Alison Chandler, "SAT Reading Scores Drop to Lowest Point in Decades," *Washington Post*, September 14, 2011, http://www.washingtonpost.com/local/education/sat-reading-scores-drop-to-lowest-point-in-decades/2011/09/14/gIQAdpoDTK_story.html.
2. Evgeny Morozov, "Losing Our Minds to the Web," *Prospect Magazine*, June 22, 2010, http://www.prospectmagazine.co.uk/2010/06/losing-our-minds-to-the-web/.
3. Nicholas Carr, "Author Nicholas Carr: The Web Shatters Focus, Rewires Brains," Wired.com, May 24, 2010, http://www.wired.com/magazine/2010/05/ff_nicholas_carr/all/1.
4. David Derbyshire, "Social Websites Harm Children's Brains: Chilling Warning to Parents from Top Neuroscientist," *Daily Mail*, February 24, 2009, http://www.dailymail.co.uk/news/article-1153583/Social-websites-harm-childrens-brains-Chilling-warning-parents-neuroscientist.html.
5. Francesca Borgonovi, "What Can Parents Do to Help Their

Children Succeed in School?," *Pisa in Focus* 10 (November 2011), http://www.pisa.oecd.org/dataoecd/4/1/49012097.pdf.

6. Ibid.

7. Ibid., emphasis mine.

8. Francesca Borgonovi, "What Can Parents Do to Help Their Children Succeed in School?," *Pisa in Focus* 10 (November 2011), http://www.pisa.oecd.org/dataoecd/4/1/49012097.pdf.

9. Thomas L. Friedman, "How about Better Parents," *New York Times*, November 19, 2011, http://www.nytimes.com/2011/11/20/opinion/sunday/friedman-how-about-better-parents.html.

10. Patte Barth, "Most Effective Parental Involvement," *American School Board Journal*, November 2011, http://www.asbj.com/MainMenuCategory/Archive/2011/November/Most-Effective-Parental-Involvement.html.

11. Joel R. Montgomery, Wikispaces.com, May 27, 2009, http://joelmonty.wikispaces.com/file/view/Using+Audio+Books+to+Improve+Academic+Performance.pdf.

12. Justine Derrick, "Using Comics with ESL/EFL Students," *Internet TESL Journal* 14, no. 7 (July 7, 2008), http://iteslj.org/Techniques/Derrick-UsingComics.html.

13. Stephen Krashen, "The 'Decline' of Reading in America," Books and Articles by Stephen D Krashen, February 2005, http://www.sdkrashen.com/articles/decline_of_reading/all.html.

14. Ibid.

15. Margaret Rudiger, "Reading Lessons: Graphic Novels 101," The Horn Book, 2005, http://archive.hbook.com/pdf/articles/mar06_rudiger.pdf.

16. Stephen Krashen, "The 'Decline' of Reading in America." Books and Articles by Stephen D Krashen, February 2005, http://www.sdkrashen.com/articles/decline_of_reading/all.html.

SLEEP

"There was never a child so lovely but his mother was glad to get him to sleep."

Ralph Waldo Emerson

CHILDREN NEED SLEEP. IT IS THE FIRST LAW OF PARENTing, and indeed the first principle along with feeding, that we focus on in those hazy, hormonal first weeks of parenthood. If children do not sleep, neither do parents, and sleep-deprived parents quickly go from their best, most patient selves to irritable, weaker copies. To the crying preschooler demanding, "Why do I have to go to bed? I'm not tired!" many a parent has replied, "Because *I* am tired."

Research shows that "across the board, parents [are] more likely to report insufficient sleep than adults without children. And moms mentioned insufficient sleep more often than dads."[1] Duh. Chasing sleep—for myself, my husband, and the children—has been a nagging, constant consideration when scheduling our lives since we became parents.

The National Sleep Foundation has published the following recommendations for optimum number of hours of sleep per twenty-four hours, according to age:

Newborns: 10.5–18 hours; *infants (3–11 months)*: 11–15

hours; *toddlers (1–3 years)*: 12–14 hours, with naps consolidated to 1 per day at around 18 months; *preschoolers (3–5 years)*: 11–13 hours (and most need no nap after the age of 5); and *five- to twelve-year-olds*: 10–11 hours.[2] This last group is known for having prevalent sleep problems.

Teens, who are supposed to have 9 hours of sleep per night, usually do not get that amount, and it is well-known that a sleep-deprived individual would do best not to get behind the wheel. Parents should strongly consider confiscating car keys from their sleep-deprived children of driving age because "young adults are responsible for more than half of the 100,000 'fall asleep' crashes annually" in the United States.[3]

Before we had kids, my husband and I liked to talk about all the things we would do with our children, what we would never do, and so forth. You know how it is; for any parenting conundrum needing answers, never turn to seasoned parents for help but rather consult those childless couples who know it all. There is a special angel in heaven, I think, whose sole purpose is to keep track of all the yet-to-be parents' statements that begin with "When *I* have kids, they will *never* . . ." or "I will make sure *my* children *always* . . ." That angel then ensures that we have ample opportunity to put our maxims to the test—which will help us gain the divine attribute of humility along the way.

Well, I can't even remember all the promises I made to and about my unborn children, but I do remember that the vision I had of being a parent was filled with creative activities, learning, games, discussions, crafting, camping, hiking, chores, reading, and the list goes on. For some reason, it was not so filled with grocery shopping, cooking, cleaning, and doing laundry. And I never knew that the greatest enemy to all my lofty pursuits was going to be *sleep*: the need for and lack of.

As a parent, I came to understand the full meaning and truth of the scripture, "retire to thy bed early, that ye may not be weary; arise early, that your bodies and your minds may be invigorated."[4] Is it sacrilegious of me to want to tweak that scripture to read, "retire to thy bed early, *and stay asleep the whole night*, that ye may not be weary . . ."? Though no doubt my insertion is already implied in the original verse.

My first parenting experience was an awakening—pun intended. Our first baby did not sleep through the night until he was five and a half—*years*. Our second child was the opposite and slept through the night when she was just two months, but add two younger siblings to that, and I can honestly say that there was a period of eight years that I never got a full night's sleep. I know my story is not unique. Sleep deprivation is very real for most parents, at least for a period of time.

And there is need for concern when it comes to sleep in our families. Apparently, our lifestyles do not accommodate enough of it. Estimates in 2006 said that 50 to 70 million Americans are chronically affected, suffering from "disorder[s] of sleep and wakefulness, hindering daily functioning," which is disquieting, since the numbers are unlikely to have gone down since then, and because "the cumulative long-term effects of sleep loss and sleep disorders have been associated with a wide range of deleterious health consequences including an increased risk of hypertension, diabetes, obesity, depression, heart attack and stroke."[5]

I am always impressed by my dad, who, when ten o'clock rolls around, starts getting ready for bed so he can function well the next day. I wish I had more of his discipline. I am prone to be a night owl.

Regarding the rising generation, in 2011 the Institute of Medicine also reported that "evidence suggests a decrease in sleep duration across infancy, childhood and adolescence over the last 20 years, with the most pronounced decreases among children under three years of age."[6] Screen time is listed as one of the culprits and will be discussed shortly, but whatever the reason for this loss of sleep, parents should take it seriously because "mounting epidemiologic evidence indicates that short duration of sleep is a risk factor for obesity among all age groups, including infants and children under the age of five."[7]

More than one study has linked lack of sleep with the increase of childhood obesity in America. Dr. Eve Van Cauter at the University of Chicago conducted research that concludes that there is "an increased risk of weight gain and obesity in children and young adults who are short sleepers. Altogether, the evidence points to a possible role of decreased sleep duration in the current epidemic of obesity."[8] The study goes into more detail than I am able to easily interpret, but one of the findings is that being sleep deprived causes a range of hormonal upsets in the body. The hormone ghrelin, which signals hunger, is increased when we are sleep deprived, the hormone leptin, which suppresses appetite, is decreased. Sleep loss also elevates the stress hormone cortisol, which stimulates the body to make fat. (Ah, so that explains why those last pounds from the final pregnancy have lingered.)

Regarding the ills of television before bed, I had my own sample of the practice recently. When a pair of sweet siblings, a girl and a boy ages eight and six, spent the night at our house, they were so wakeful at bedtime I had to repeatedly go into the room and ask them to settle down. In the bedroom next door, our own three oldest children were asleep at 8:30 p.m.

"We're used to watching TV at night," the little boy complained at 9:30 p.m. "How come you don't have a TV in any of the bedrooms?"

"Because it is not good for children's brains to watch TV right before bed," I replied. "It makes it hard for kids to sleep well at night."

"I believe that," said the eight-year old girl. "Because every night when I watch TV, my eyes get really wide like this"—she opened her eyes wide—"and it makes me really awake. It takes a long time for me to fall asleep."

When I turned on the audiobook version of *The Lion, the Witch and the Wardrobe* by C. S. Lewis, I learned that these kids had never before listened to an audiobook. But they were familiar with the story because they had seen the movie, and they eagerly listened. Unfortunately, I think this unbalanced relationship with books and TV is rather common among American children today.

The increased screen time that has been associated with loss of sleep has prompted the Institute of Medicine to recommend for health care providers to "counsel parents and other caregivers of children not to place televisions and other media in young children's bedrooms."[9]

Dr. Michele M. Garrison, researcher at Seattle Children's Research Institute, reports results from a study of six hundred children between three and five years old that observed "sleep problems in preschool-aged children for each additional hour of daytime violent media content or evening media use. The types of sleep problems reported by parents included trouble falling asleep, nightmares, waking during the night, trouble with morning alertness, and daytime sleepiness. The majority of violent media exposure in this study was from children's programming, rather than programming intended for adults or adolescents."[10]

Effects of not getting enough sleep, for children and adults alike, with which parents are likely to be familiar have to do with controlling emotions. "The part of the brain that helps us control our actions and our response to feelings is affected greatly by lack of sleep. Not getting enough sleep can lead to all kinds of problems, such as behavior problems, attention problems, and not doing well in school."[11]

Insufficient sleep among high school students has been linked to the following health risk behaviors: "non-diet soda consumption; lack of physical activity; hours spent watching television; hours spent playing video or computer games or using a computer for a reason not related to school work; use of cigarettes, alcohol, or marijuana; sexual intercourse; feelings of sadness or hopelessness; and serious consideration of suicide."[12] Students who reported insufficient sleep had "higher odds of engaging in the risk behavior than did students who reported sufficient sleep."[13] If we can combat a list of such undesirable behaviors by simply encouraging more sleep, then that is good news to me.

In 2006, over the course of a week, high school students missed 11.7 hours of sleep, and their parents were mostly in the dark about it. When polled, nine out of ten parents believed that their teens got an adequate amount of sleep at least a few nights of the week, but this is not the reality. Says the National Sleep Foundation, "At least once a week, more than one-quarter of high school students fall asleep in school, 22% fall asleep doing homework, and 14% arrive late or miss school because they oversleep. 80% of adolescents who get an optimal amount of sleep say they're achieving As and Bs in school, while adolescents who get insufficient amounts of sleep are more likely than their peers to get lower grades."[14]

Some of the most compelling research linking sleep and school performance was done by Dr. Avi Sadeh, a clinical psychologist at Tel Aviv University. Dr. Sadeh tested seventy-seven nine- and eleven-year-olds after three nights of either thirty minutes more sleep or thirty minutes less than optimum. The results were astonishing. An eleven-year-old child with three days of thirty minutes less sleep performed at a nine-year-old level. "A loss of one hour of sleep is equivalent to [the loss of] two years of cognitive maturation and development," Sadeh explained.[15]

Having learned this, I was thrilled when my son came home from school in third grade clutching the October 8, 2010, issue of *Time for Kids*, and the cover said, "Kids Need More Sleep." The article inside explained all about how good and bad sleep habits relate to academic performance and also how it affects mood—using kid-friendly language. I kept that copy to use it on bedtime-resistant members of our household.

But our children's most powerful lesson about sleep did not come from *Time for Kids*. Our oldest daughter has been diagnosed with epilepsy. The first time she suffered two serious, back-to-back, prolonged, grand mal seizures was early in the morning after a hectic week of little sleep in the beginning of December. I did not associate the many late nights during Thanksgiving break with her seizures until, after nine months of no seizures, she suffered another, this time in August after late nights of water adventures, miniature golf, and drive-in movies. After the second incident, I saw the relationship immediately, being intimately familiar with other effects of sleep loss on my own brain.

Indeed, Elina's pediatric neurologist confirmed the connection between sleep loss and epileptic seizures when I asked about it. And Steven C. Schachter, MD, from the Epilepsy Therapy Project, writes, "Some people suffer a single seizure for the only time in their entire life after an 'all-nighter' at college or after a prolonged period of poor sleep associated with a major life stress. If you have epilepsy, lack of proper sleep can increase your chance of having a seizure. It can even increase the intensity and length of seizures."[16] This tells me that the impact of sleep deprivation on the brain is a serious one.

Because of Elina's illness, we now take sleep very seriously in our house. The cumulative effect of sleep loss seems to be a particular trigger, and she has gotten away with a solitary late night here and there. But our approach to sleep (for her especially) is to keep a consistent, early bedtime and make up occasional lost sleep. On Halloween, for instance, when I know that trick-or-treating and the party afterward will be energy-zapping and late, I make all the kids take a nap earlier in the day. And if Elina wakes up with an allergy attack in the middle of the night that keeps her up, I often let her sleep in the next morning and take her to school an hour or so later to prevent that cumulative deficit of sleep that may trigger a seizure.

Some longtime friends of ours, a married couple with two children, make sleep a higher priority than many families I have seen. When their children were toddlers and church interfered with their nap time, one of the parents would stay home so the sleep schedule would not be disturbed. I thought the measure a bit extreme sometimes, but after wrangling my own delirious toddler out of an undesired late nap and dealing with ensuing late bedtime as well as Monday's fragmented sleep schedule, I often wished that our church congregation would always meet at 9:00 a.m. rather than be subjected to the yearly rotation of 11:00 a.m. or 1:00 p.m. with the two other congregations that use the same building.

When we had our sleep-prioritizing friends and their children (eight and six years old at the time) over for New Year's Eve (before I discovered the sleep/epilepsy connection), I expected to ring in the new year at midnight with them (and whatever children had managed to stay awake), but at 7:45 p.m., the parents gave their children the 'ten-minute warning,' and by 8:00 p.m. they were gone.

"It is already past their bedtime, you know," the dad explained as they put their shoes on. "And sleep is everything. It is absolutely *key* to children's development."

But it's New Year's Eve! I thought to myself and fondly recalled the New Year's Eves of my childhood in Narvik, Norway, staying up as late as I possibly could, watching the televised "year-in-review," and setting off fireworks at midnight along with the rest of the town.

Seeing my facial expression, our friend explained further, referring to a minor crying incident that happened with their daughter at 7:30 p.m. "That was a sign that it was past bedtime. It would never have happened an hour earlier, plus tomorrow will be ruined if we stay up too late."

Though I didn't feel that way at the time, the more I have learned about the importance of sleep, the more obvious it is to me that our sleep-committed friends are not off the mark. Luckily, it is always midnight somewhere in the world, so we can watch fireworks online from London, Paris, or Stockholm early in the evening on New Year's Eve, wish each other a happy new year, and then send the kids to bed.

Now, if only Mom and Dad could learn to tuck themselves in too, as opposed to staying up late and watching movies, we wouldn't be so desperate for that New Year's Day nap.

Notes

1. Miranda Hitti, "Sleep Deprivation Common in Parents," WebMD, May 23, 2007, http://www.webmd.com/parenting /news/20070523/sleep-deprivation-common-in-parents.
2. "Children and Sleep," National Sleep Foundation, accessed January 2, 2012, http://www.sleepfoundation.org/article /sleep-topics/children-and-sleep.

3. Po Bronson and Ashley Merryman, "The Lost Hour," in *NurtureShock: New Thinking about Children* (New York: Twelve, 2009), 27–44.

4. Doctrine and Covenants 88:124.

5. "Sleep Disorders and Sleep Deprivation: An Unmet Public Health Problem," Institute of Medicine, March 21, 2006, http://www.iom.edu/Reports/2006/Sleep-Disorders-and-Sleep -Deprivation-An-Unmet-Public-Health-Problem.aspx.

6. Institute of Medicine, "Early Childhood Obesity Prevention Policies," report, June 23, 2011, http://www.iom.edu /Reports/2011/Early-Childhood-Obesity-Prevention-Policies /Report-Brief.aspx?page=2.

7. Ibid.

8. Eve Van Cauter and Kristen L. Knutson, "Sleep and the Epidemic of Obesity in Children and Adults," supplement, *European Journal of Endocrinology* 159, no. S1 (December 1, 2008): S59–66, doi:10.1530/EJE-08-0298.

9. Institute of Medicine, "Early Childhood Obesity Prevention Policies," report, June 23, 2011, http://www.iom.edu /Reports/2011/Early-Childhood-Obesity-Prevention-Policies /Report-Brief.aspx?page=2.

10. Seattle Children's Hospital, Seattle Children's Research Institute, "Studies Examine Impact of Media Use among Youth," news release, June 27, 2011, http://www.seattlechildrens .org/press-releases/2011/studies-examine-impact-of-media-use -among-youth,-recommend-preventative-measures/.

11. Kyla Boyse, "Sleep Problems: Your Child," University of Michigan Health System, November 2010, http://www.med .umich.edu/yourchild/topics/sleep.htm.

12. Leslie Sinclair, "Teens Lack of Sleep Linked with Health-Risk Behaviors," *Psychiatric News*, December 2, 2011, http://psych news.psychiatryonline.org/newsarticle.aspx?articleid=180868.

13. Ibid.

14. National Sleep Foundation, 2006 *Sleep in America* Poll Highlights and Key Findings, accessed January 2, 2012, http://www.sleepfoundation.org/sites/default/files/Highlights _facts_06.pdf.

15. Po Bronson and Ashley Merryman, "The Lost Hour," in

NurtureShock: New Thinking about Children (New York: Twelve, 2009), 27–44.

16. Steven C. Schachter, "Sleep Deprivation and Epilepsy," Epilepsy Therapy Project, December 15, 2006, http://www.epilepsy.com /epilepsy/provoke_sleepdep.

FACEBOOK

"Don't say anything online that you wouldn't want plastered on a billboard with your face on it."

Erin Bury

YOU HAVE A FACEBOOK ACCOUNT. ADMIT IT. IF YOU ARE not one of the nine hundred million people who have a Facebook account,[1] then I applaud and envy you. I want to be you. Or, at least, I wish I could be more like my dad, who logs in once a month and never posts anything.

I once deactivated my account for a whole semester. Why? Because when I was on Facebook, I wanted to log off. I needed to log off. I intended to log off. I only signed in to read a message, but thirty minutes later, I was still there, for the third time that day! I have never played Farmville or Farkle (in fact, I blocked all such applications from day one), but I would get caught in a spiral of interesting articles to read, funny video clips, and people's pictures. I couldn't control my time. And from the looks of statistics, I am not alone.

Each Facebook user spends on average fifteen hours and thirty-three minutes a month on the site.[2] Imagine what wonders I could have accomplished with that extra time. In fact, according to recent statistics, social networking now comprises twice as much of our online time as any other activity.[3] Is this the cause for the downturn in our economy? Are we so unproductive as a people, playing mindless Facebook games and scrolling down the newsfeed of what people made for dinner, that it hampers our ability to do our work well? To say nothing of how it poses a significant hurdle in the way we interact in society and our families. Well, regardless of what is to blame for our economic and societal problems, I concluded that Facebook was hampering my productivity, so I sent myself to rehab by deactivating my account. And I explained why to my family.

In the end, with my immediate and extended family all living across the ocean, I just missed the gateway to their lives too much to bid Facebook farewell forever, so after that semester, I reactivated the account and found that I was better at controlling my time. But as I write this, my Facebook account is once again shut down, so you can guess if that newfound control of my time lasted forever . . .

Social media is not inherently bad, of course. But it is certainly a love-hate relationship for me. I don't dare get an iPhone or any of its cousins for fear that I would get sucked into it and all its apps (Facebook at the top of the list) and lose sight of the life I am living or chip away at the real-time connections I want to have with my immediate family. I have seen too many parents at various outings (parks, museums, the zoo, and so on), bent over their cell phones, feverishly texting or scrolling down the newsfeed while missing time and experiences with their kids. My long-held "fear" of the smartphone was validated when the Smith School of Business at the University of Maryland came out with two studies concluding that our cell phones make us more selfish and less likely to behave in a pro-social manner.[4] This is only a working study and has not been peer-reviewed, so more research is needed in this area about how our smartphone usage is affecting our behavior and relationships.

But back to Facebook. I wish there were a twenty-minute time limit application available—one that kicks me off when the time is up and wouldn't allow me back until the next day or week. But with revenue from ads powering the site, I cannot imagine that such a feature will ever be available.

And it isn't just Facebook and social media. Controlling time and activity online, no matter what the site, is not easy. This new era requires parents to be savvy, not just about using the Internet but also about the negative effects it can have on its users. Kids are especially vulnerable. Dangers are lurking online. So we teach them about password safety, to not divulge personal information, to not blindly click on links, and so forth. These are among the essential skills.

But did you know kids have to be thirteen or older to legally have a Facebook account? US Congress passed the Children's Online Privacy Protection Act (COPPA) in 1998, which requires commercial websites to obtain parental permission before collecting the personal information of any user under thirteen. Most websites find it too costly and cumbersome to do, so they simply place an age limit.[5] But this age limit is ignored by millions. Every day, kids lie to create their profiles, and parents are largely indifferent to it or ignorant about the age limit in the first place. Among those parents who do know about the age limit, almost all are unaware as to the real reason for restricting children's access (namely COPPA). When asked in a recent survey, only 2 out of 1007 parents of ten- to thirteen-year-olds answered correctly.[6] Most parents think it is because Facebook is designed for adults and therefore not appropriate for kids, as well as due to the risk for exposure to online predators, and so forth—all of which is real and should be reason enough for parents to think twice before letting children enter the Facebook realm.

But it doesn't hurt to teach kids a thing or two about how social media works before they become users. One thing that we have tried to be mindful of in our family is to not post pictures of or status updates about the kids that might embarrass them. And we don't post anything without their knowledge—even the young ones, as much as that is possible. I feel it is so important to respect their privacy as my equals and not to exploit or objectify their cuteness, no matter how well-intended.

"Internet benefits and risks" seems to be a lesson worth focusing on with our children. My son and daughter, who are still in elementary school, ride the school bus home most days, and a surprising number of their peers are equipped with both iPhones and iPads—devices that quickly become the center of attention on the bus ride home. Kids are clustered around the games, pictures, and underage Facebook profiles, much to my dismay. When discussing this issue with a classmate (a mother of three) in my graduate program, she sighed.

"I'm not worried about Facebook," she said. "My six-year-old was exposed to porn via a third-grade neighbor on the school bus because he had a smartphone on which he accessed these things."

Stories like these are enough to make anyone want to march into the superintendent's office and demand a no-electronics rule on any school property, the bus included.

Sometimes Facebook users highlight the exciting aspects of their lives (I know I have), and other times Facebook becomes a venting forum. There is another good reason for parents to filter what we share about our kids online. I hope they will appreciate this effort and that our showing them this respect means that they will return it to us when in the future they are users of social media. I do not want pictures of myself floating around the Internet—especially those snapped by my children some morning of me, with yesterday's makeup and a frizzy ponytail, making toast in the kitchen. I also hope our restraint teaches them to be cautious online sharers about their own lives.

Of course, it is possible to limit the number of "friends" who see certain posts. I have certainly made use of these privacy features. But I find it difficult to explain to the kids. I know they are smart enough to understand how many of these things work if I were to take the time to do it. But I am worried about the sort of slippery slope it would create. Instead my aim is to steer them away from Facebook as much as possible and to teach them that sharing less information and spending less time on Facebook—and online, period—is better.

According to a *Consumer Reports* survey, there are approximately 7.5 million underage Facebook users. Five million of them are under ten. Their online activity is largely unsupervised, and most of their parents are unconcerned.[7] It is strange that in a day and age when most kids are not allowed to ride their bikes unsupervised to the next neighborhood, many are given free rein online for hours at a time.

Getting an underage Facebook profile removed without parental involvement is next to impossible. Anyone can report an underage user anonymously, but the forum for doing so is not easy to find. And then the Facebook team must be able to verify with certainty that the user is under thirteen. This means that most underage users are safe as long as their own parents do not turn them in.

Founder of Facebook, Mark Zuckerberg, does not hide the fact that the Facebook team wants to eliminate the age limit. "My philosophy is that for education you need to start at a really, really young age," he says. "Because of the [age] restrictions we haven't even begun this learning process. If they're lifted then we'd start to learn what works. We'd take a lot of precautions to make sure that they [younger kids] are safe."[8]

I question Zuckerberg's motives here. What sort of education are children subjected to when they are freely allowed on social media websites? I can't help but think that the marketing and money-making potential is the real lure here, not the educational interests of the children.

The *Wall Street Journal* reported in June 2012 that "Facebook is developing technology that would allow children younger than 13 years old to use the social-networking site under parental supervision." These new mechanisms would allow parents to connect their children's accounts to their own and to have a say in whom their kids are allowed to "friend" as well as in what applications they can use. These "under-13 features could enable Facebook and its partners to charge parents for games and other entertainment accessed by their children." It remains to be seen whether this technology will be launched.[9]

Though reports of online bullying and predators are alarming, we don't need to assume that all kids are harmed this dramatically by their online activity. The risk of feeling some effects of online bullying are real for most young users, but there are other consequences. Scientists say that "our ability to focus is being undermined by bursts of information. The stimulation provokes excitement—a dopamine squirt—that can be addictive. In its absence, people feel bored."[10] Research also shows that the glorified ability to multitask is not only falsely placed on a pedestal, it is a myth. Heavy multitaskers are not more effective. Instead, they experience more stress and have more trouble focusing and ignoring irrelevant information.[11] (This would explain why I can't serve a snack, help with homework, and unload dishes at the same time with any degree of efficiency).

Clifford Nass, professor at Stanford University, said that during a study of heavy Internet multitaskers, researchers discovered that the heavy multitaskers were much more easily distracted. They also had significantly less control over their working memory, and their ability to focus on a task was diminished. According to Nass, intensive multitaskers are "suckers for irrelevancy. Everything distracts them."[12] Michael Merzenich, professor emeritus neuroscientist at the University of California, San Francisco, went a bit further and said that multitasking online is "training our brains to pay attention to the crap."[13]

The American Psychological Association reports that "multitasking may seem efficient on the surface but may actually take more time in the end and involve more error" because "even brief mental blocks created by shifting between tasks can cost as much as 40 percent of someone's productive time."[14]

Sue Palmer, author of *Toxic Childhood*, said: "We are seeing children's brain development damaged because they don't engage in the activity they have engaged in for millennia."[15] I presume she is referring to such nearly outdated activities as unstructured play, outdoor activity, working/doing chores alongside their parents, and having conversations with other humans (face-to-face).

A growing number of psychologists and neuroscientists believe these social media sites may be doing more harm than good, especially to young children. Baroness Greenfield, an Oxford University neuroscientist and director of the Royal Institution, believes repeated exposure can effectively "rewire" the brain, especially those of young children.[16]

And it is true, the human brain can actually rewire itself

at any age. This is consistent with the belief of many of the dominant religions, that we can repent, change, and become something new. In the scientific community the term *brain plasticity* is used, referring to how the brain reorganizes itself in response to how we engage with the world around us. The website CogniFit, (a site designed for people to explore their brains and assess their cognitive skills) writes that, "brain plasticity is the reason scientifically validated brain fitness training is effective. Brain plasticity may also mean that using obsessively social media networks could have unintended consequences for our brains and cognitive skills."[17]

Specifically, our attention span has been shown to suffer as a result of heavy social media use and online multitasking. A recent survey conducted by Lloyds TSB Insurance Services in the United Kingdom suggests that attention spans have gone from twelve to just five minutes over the last ten years. Not surprisingly, young people are the worst at maintaining concentration.[18]

These declining attention spans can cause real harm, the same study shows, since they have been linked to household accidents. Food boiling over on the stove, overflowing bathtubs, and freezer doors left open are among them. In the survey, 25 percent of the participants said they regularly forget the names of close friends or relatives, and 7 percent even admitted to momentarily forgetting their own birthdays.

Worthy of note, however, is that the people over fifty years old had superior abilities to concentrate compared to younger people. This suggests that the heavy use of modern technology is at least in part to blame for our cognitive decline. Surely we will want to spare ourselves and our children this unfortunate side effect of technology use by mastering technology and our time before technology masters us.

In addition, recent studies have pointed to the tendency for online users of all ages to become desensitized in interactions with others. Our empathy—one of our greatest human traits—can easily become hampered as we interact with others through social media. If we would like to raise children with this worthy attribute, we would do well to reconsider the amount of time spent using Facebook, in favor of fostering face-to-face relations.

Communications professor Clifford Nass from Stanford University claims that our heavy use of technology alters the way we interact with each other and that the caring aspect of relationships goes missing when we rely heavily on technology.[19]

Bree Barton, for *USA Today*, takes it a step further and argues that "posting a Tweet or updating a Facebook status isn't real engagement. It's narcissism masquerading as connection. The anonymity of the Internet drives a wedge between our true self and our virtual persona, enabling us to disassociate from the consequences our actions have on others."[20] And perhaps she is right.

In any case, I expect striving for balance in technology use is going to be a constant endeavor for my family because technology is not going away. There is no one-size-fits-all solution that can be applied to all families, nor can any solution be expected to apply to the same family over time. But for now, for our family, it does include one computer, centrally located; rather strict time limits for use (for the kids especially); certainly no underage Facebook accounts; a periodic shutdown of my own Facebook account; no smartphones; and an ongoing attempt at being engaged in nonvirtual activities. I assume we are not alone in this battle against a virtual childhood, even if choices about exactly how to go about the struggle will vary from family to family.

Notes

1. Anton Troianovski and Shayndi Raice, "Facebook Explores Giving Kids Access," *Wall Street Journal*, June 4, 2012, http://online.wsj.com/article/SB1000142405270230350640457744447 11741019238.html.

2. Ibid.

3. Adam Ostrow, "Social Networking Dominates Our Time Spent Online [STATS]," The Social Media Guide, August 2, 2010, http://mashable.com/2010/08/02/stats-time-spent-online/.

4. "Cellphone Use Linked to Selfish Behavior in Smith Marketing Study," Robert H. Smith School of Business, accessed March 20, 2012, http://www.rhsmith.umd.edu/news/stories/2012 /CellPhoneStudy.aspx.

5. Helen A. S. Popkin, "Kids Still Lie to Get on Facebook, Parents Still Okay with That," November 1, 2011, http://digitallife .today.msnbc.msn.com/_news/2011/11/01/8581244-kids-still -lie-to-get-on-facebook-parents-still-ok-with-that.

6. Ibid.

7. "Facebook Concerns," *Consumer Reports*, June 2011, http://www.consumerreports.org/cro/magazine-archive/2011/june /electronics-computers/state-of-the-net/facebook-concerns /index.htm.

8. Emil Protalinksi, "Mark Zuckerberg: Facebook Minimum Age Limit Should Be Removed," ZDNet, May 20, 2011, http://www.zdnet.com/blog/facebook/mark-zuckerberg-facebook -minimum-age-limit-should-be-removed/1506.

9. Anton Troianovski and Shayndi Raice, "Facebook Explores Giving Kids Access," *Wall Street Journal*, June 4, 2012, http://online.wsj.com/article/SB1000142405270230350640457744447 11741019238.html.

10. Matt Richtel, "Attached to Technology and Paying a Price," *New York Times*, June 6, 2010, http://www.nytimes.com/2010/06/07 /technology/07brain.html?emc=eta1&pagewanted=all.

11. Ibid.

12. Adam Gorlick, "Media Multitaskers Pay Mental Price, Stanford Study Shows," Stanford University News, August 24, 2009, http://news.stanford.edu/news/2009/august24/multitask -research-study-082409.html.

13. Nicholas Carr, "Author Nicholas Carr: The Web Shatters Focus, Rewires Brains," *Wired Magazine*, May 24, 2010, http://www .wired.com/magazine/2010/05/ff_nicholas_carr/all/1.

14. "Multitasking: Switching Costs," *American Psychological Association*, March 20, 2006, http://www.apa.org/research /action/multitask.aspx.

15. David Derbyshire, "Social Websites Harm Children's Brains: Chilling Warning to Parents from Top Neuroscientist," *Daily Mail*, February 24, 2009, http://www.dailymail.co.uk /news/article-1153583/Social-websites-harm-childrens-brains -Chilling-warning-parents-neuroscientist.html.

16. Ibid.

17. "Is Social Media Affecting Our Brains?," CogniFit's Blog, June 22, 2011, http://blog.cognifit.com/2011/06/is-social-media -affecting-our-brains.html.

18. Matthew Moore, "Stress of Modern Life Cuts Attention Spans to Five Minutes—Telegraph," Telegraph.co.uk, November 26, 2008, http://www.telegraph.co.uk/health/healthnews/3522781 /Stress-of-modern-life-cuts-attention-spans-to-five-minutes .html.

19. Marianne LeVine, "Technology: Does It Breed or Kill Empathy?" Stanford Daily, October 28, 2010, http://www.stanforddaily .com/2010/10/28/technology-does-it-breed-or-kill-empathy/.

20. Keith Simmons, "In Our Social Media World, Is Empathy Dying?," USA Today, October 19, 2010, http://www.usatoday .com/news/opinion/forum/2010-10-20-column20_ST1_N .htm.

OUTDOOR PLAY

"Forget not that the earth delights to feel your bare feet
and the winds long to play with your hair."

Kahlil Gibran

I CONSIDER THE COUNTLESS HOURS I HAVE SPENT IN unstructured play, unsupervised outside, to be the jewel of my childhood and certainly one of the greatest blessings of my life. And we have thus reached the topic of this book that is most likely to make me break down in tears. In fact, after reading the wonderful book *Last Child in the Woods* by Richard Louv with my nonfiction book club four years ago, I actually *did* cry when it was my turn to add my thoughts. But I had just given birth to my third baby. I am sure I was hormonal.

Please know that it is not my intent to make any of us cry. But let us consider the picture of American childhood today and do something to rescue our children from the worst effects of it: "Today, childhood is spent mostly indoors, watching television, playing video games and working the Internet. When children do go outside, it tends to be for scheduled events—soccer camp or a fishing derby—held under the watch of adults. In a typical week, 27% of kids ages 9 to 13 play organized baseball, but only

6% play on their own."[1] Surely we can do better than this without risking their physical safety.

Since the 1970s, children's free time has declined by twelve hours per week, and unstructured outdoor activities have fallen by 50 percent. In addition, there has been a 25 percent decrease in play, according to Dr. Romina Barros, leader of a research team at the Albert Einstein College of Medicine at Yeshiva University.[2]

As a young child I roamed my grandparents' large farm freely on my weekend visits, along with many unfettered animals. I was three years old when an aggressive rooster attacked me by jumping me from behind and digging his sharp claws through my jeans and shirt. *Twice*! I managed to run away until he no longer followed me and then caught my breath. I cried. My heart beat madly in my chest. But under no circumstance would I tell my grandmother about the incident for fear that she might deem it too dangerous for me to be outside by myself in the future. Instead, I would just be doubly careful to avoid that wretched rooster.

A year or so later, I got butted by a ram right in the kidneys so hard I flew through the air and ate dirt when I landed. I didn't cry then. I *screamed*. It happened outside the dining room window of the farmhouse, and my uncle Erik saw it. To my intense relief, I was not forbidden to go outside after that incident. I was just given a brief warning to keep a good eye on the old ram. And so I did.

My outside adventures were not limited to the countryside. I actually grew up in town, where my friend Josef and I "owned" the city center. Together with other kids in the area, we played so long and hard outside that when I finally made it home, my body ached from hunger and fatigue. Sure, we did things we should not have done. But sometimes they provided the most learning—at least in the long run.

We stole apples from the branches of other peoples' trees, felt the rush of adrenaline as we tried to run away unseen, and experienced the guilt when my mother asked us "if stolen apples tasted as good as those honestly purchased." And I can add that Josef should *never, ever* have walked on the parapet wall on the roof of that five-story building downtown—a feat I was against then and am just thankful he survived. We also shouldn't have disturbed the creaking attic of a certain historic apartment building, but we did it repeatedly just to experience the thrill of the old Russian woman chasing us out. But 90 percent of the time, we were simply engaged in some fantasy adventure game that lasted for hours and would continue the next day and the next. And when we got too hungry and didn't want to go home, we collected recycling or played our recorders for money so we could buy pizza.

On weekends when I was not at my grandmother's farm, I often roamed deep into the woods where my parents were building our summer house—a house that we would later add on to and use as our primary residence. With my Labrador retriever for companionship, I found every trail in the dense forest and got very lost a couple of times.

On longer school breaks I usually went to see my grandparents in Norway, above the Arctic Circle. My friend Jorunn and I liked to climb the little forest-clad hill in town and jump over the old World War II trenches as we made our way up. We rode our bikes all over the city, played at the harbor, sunned ourselves on the top of the terrifyingly tall diving tower by the beach in the summer, and in the winter built snowmen in the dark until we could no longer feel our fingers. To say nothing of the countless days spent on my grandfather's fishing boat, taking in the breathtaking views of the fjord and mountains, catching fish until dawn (sometimes) in the perpetually sunlit arctic summers.

The fondness I feel for my outside adventures as a child is not unique. According to research, "when asked to name the most significant place from their childhood, adults consistently named an outdoor place."[3] Don't we want our kids to do the same?

Yet children spend less and less time engaged in outdoor play. America is not alone in this. In Europe, "young people now face heart problems, diabetes and other diseases because of their sedentary lifestyles."[4] In the United States, children have low levels of vitamin D—about 70 percent are actually vitamin D deficient, which puts them at higher risk for bone and heart disease.[5] The cause? Poor diet and lack of sunshine.

Says Dr. Michal Melamed, at the Albert Einstein College of Medicine at Yeshiva University, "It would be good for [parents] to turn off the TV and send their kids outside. Just 15 to 20 minutes a day should be enough. And unless they burn easily, don't put sunscreen on them until they've been out in the sun for 10 minutes, so they get the good stuff but not sun damage."[6] Dr. Melamed goes on to explain that vitamin D is not, in fact, a vitamin, but a hormone that has important functions in the body. Vitamin D can help reduce chances of heart disease and cancer, performs vital functions for the immune system, can alleviate depression, reduces acne, and may also help with weight loss. The list goes on and on.

In contrast, Vitamin D deficiency can result in the bone disease rickets, which has been found in children in increasing numbers in recent years.[7] It is difficult to get vitamin D via diet but easy to get it through fifteen to twenty minutes of sun exposure per day.

I think the main reason parents are reluctant to let their children outside to play unsupervised these days is the fear of stranger danger. But there are ways that we can provide lots more outdoor activity for kids without structuring them to death. Walking to school, for example, is something a lot more kids can do.

According to information gathered by the Pedestrian and Bicycle Information Center (PBIC) in collaboration with Safe Routes to School (SRTS), "in 1969, 48 percent of children 5 to 14 years of age walked or bicycled to school. In 2009, 13 percent of children 5 to 14 years of age walked or bicycled to school."[8] In many cases it is not practical to walk or bike to school. It is perhaps unsafe or the distance is too great.

But if your school district is anything like mine, many parents still drive their children to school every day even though they live less than a seven-minute walk away, and even though they do not have to be at work immediately after dropping off their kids.

One of my best friends has arranged a so-called "walking school bus" for the kids on her street and a few neighboring ones. Parents take turns walking with kids the fifteen minutes to and from school, though not all participating families can provide "drivers" because of work schedules. It is a joy to see them each morning, a throng of kids and one adult making their way chattering along the sidewalks, passing the line of stagnant cars as they move closer to the school.

When our son broke his arm after being knocked over at the skate rink (and his arm was skated over) he had to have corrective surgery, and his arm was placed in a series of splints, casts, and finally a brace. His missed his soccer season. He was not allowed to participate in PE. He had to take it easy at recess. He being a high-energy child, I worried about the lack of physical activity he would be forced to endure for ten weeks.

The solution: skipping the bus and walking to school. It

took us a good thirty minutes to walk the 1.6 miles to school each morning with four kids and a dog, and it required us to get up at 6:00 a.m. as opposed to 6:30. Frankly, I expected some resistance from the kids regarding this new routine and was prepared to defend my decision many times over. To my surprise, their enthusiasm was enormous. One time, when I had failed to set the alarm and we simply did not have time to walk, the kids were all mutinous.

It was great exercise for all of us (especially me). But the most lasting of the benefits from these walks have not been physical. We have had some of the best discussions, ever, on these walks. The act of talking and walking is therapeutic, and I have found that we have had more quality and varied discussions on the way to school than we often have around the dinner table.

And if it rained, it only added to their joy! Anja, four years old, would often say, "Mom, remember the best day of my life?"

"Which one?" I would ask.

"You know the best day of my life is always when we go walking in the rain!"

And it is true; if it rains, our kids will head outside to be in it. Every time.

Another discovery I made when I walked back to the house after dropping off the kids was how many middle schoolers live in our neighborhood. They would be out waiting for the school bus as I made my way back, and I was surprised to see that three or four kids on every corner regularly caught the bus in the mornings. I had never seen them before! I presume because they travel to and from their houses by vehicle. They certainly have never been seen riding their bikes through the neighborhood or playing outside in any fashion—not even shooting hoops in their driveways.

The day Isak finally removed his cast was the same day Elina tripped on her untied shoelaces in a parking lot and broke *her* arm. True story! (Her mother *may* have said something about tying said laces . . .) We were on our way to a pumpkin patch and farm with picnic basket prepared. Instead we spent the afternoon at the urgent care.

Another child was thus exempt from PE for several weeks. But as we moved into November, the younger kids began to grumble about it being cold in the mornings, so their enthusiasm for our morning walk withered along with my own resolve, I am quick to admit. So I certainly know why outdoor activity is not always attractive. But the oft-repeated Swedish saying "There is no bad weather, only bad clothing" convicts me. The bottom line: we need to get outside—all of us, our young ones in particular—one way or another.

When our first two children were very young, we added on to our small house. My husband did almost all the work himself to save money, and it resulted in a backyard that was dangerous for young kids to play in because of the many building materials and tools that were stored there. For a long time, any outdoor activity had to be an organized, parent-led event for our kids, and it became a form of torture for me to not be able to ever let them outside unsupervised, even in the backyard. We often rode our bikes or walked in our neighborhood and nearby nature areas, but I longed with a vengeance for an area where the kids could play daily on their own. I am thankful to be able to say that for several years now we have enjoyed such a place, and the difference it has made for our family is incalculable. My heart goes out to all the parents and children who do not find themselves in an area where they can easily enjoy the outdoors.

Obesity rates among American children are at an

all-time high. Some researchers, however, have found that the most effective way to combat the obesity epidemic may not necessarily be by structured sports or deliberate exercise, but rather by encouraging children to simply play. Because it is not seen as exercise, it has a more positive connotation than, say, riding the stationary bike.[9] What is the best form of exercise? The kind you enjoy, because that is the exercise you are most likely to stick with!

Researchers Burdette and Whitaker claim that outdoor play "is also a way children optimize their own brain development. Viewed from this perspective, the nostalgic observation that children 'no longer play' should be taken seriously because the consequences for child well-being extend beyond the problem of obesity."[10] As such, unstructured outdoor play has the potential to improve all aspects of children's well-being, including emotional, social, cognitive, and physical.

The need to provide outdoor play does not lie squarely on only parents' shoulders, however. Changes in public school practices since the No Child Left Behind Act have put recess on the back burner. But recess is badly needed, even crucial. As mentioned before, there are benefits besides the purely physical for kids to run around and play outside. According to researchers at the Albert Einstein College of Medicine at Yeshiva University, school children who receive more recess behave better and are likely to learn more, according to a large study of third graders conducted in 2009.[11]

Romina Barros, quoted at the beginning of this chapter, explains how this worrisome trend affects children in poverty the most: "We know that many disadvantaged children are not free to roam their neighborhoods, even their own yards, unless they are with an adult. Recess may be the only opportunity for these kids to practice their social skills with other children."[12] Poorly developed social skills in today's children can have disastrous effects when they become teens and adults and have not learned to problem solve, to cooperate with peers, or to properly regulate emotion and behavior.

Need more evidence? Consider these five documented benefits of nature and the outdoors:

1. Young children who frequently play outside display greater "motor coordination and attentional capacities" than those who spend less time outside.[13]

2. Children grow emotionally and academically when they engage in unstructured outdoor play.[14]

3. Girls whose home environment is a more natural one have better self-discipline. (On tests of concentration, impulse inhibition, and delay of gratification, those whose view from home was a more natural one had higher scores.)[15]

4. Children diagnosed with attention deficit/hyperactivity disorder (ADHD) or attention deficit disorder (ADD) show reduced symptoms after playing in natural areas.[16]

5. Views of nature reduce stress levels and speed recovery from illness, injury, or stressful experiences.[17]

The last point is often made by my husband, who likes to take the "scenic route" to his work. Even though it takes slightly longer, it relaxes him to drive through the pretty countryside and to be away from the traffic.

A far more in-depth treatise on this subject (of what is and is not known about the importance of nature to children's healthy development) can be found in Stephen R. Kellert's book *Building for Life*. In it he states, "Play in nature, particularly during the critical period of middle childhood [ages seven to twelve years], appears to be an especially important time for developing the capacities for creativity, problem-solving, and emotional and intellectual development."[18]

We fear for abduction and molestation that can occur as a result of kids playing outside by themselves. Such events are irreparable and unspeakable tragedies to any individual and family affected. It makes headlines when it happens and brings an emotional jolt of fear and horror to all parents when we read of them. But the slow and steady damage done to our rising generation by the absence of outdoor play is also tragic, if less sudden. If our fear of crime brings the result that children cannot enjoy any kind of unstructured play outside on a regular basis throughout their childhood, then such a childhood becomes a travesty of no small proportion.

I hope that parents and neighbors will band together to foster opportunities for children to have some semblance of the kind of childhood we had a generation or two ago. If this issue is brought a little more to the forefront of our minds, surely we could manage to turn the tide a little. Just like my friend and her walking school bus, neighbors and friends can take turns a few times per week and be present (but not overly meddling) while kids play outside—like a teacher on recess duty. Let them bring out their bikes, balls, and scooters and run around. Let them use sidewalk chalk and make hopscotches. It need not be a structured or elaborate event, but if they require some coaching in fun games to do outside, then by all means provide it.

I have seen over and over that if my children go outside to play, it usually does not take long for the neighbor kids to join them. And I always feel like they are safer, the larger the group. They certainly have more fun. Even if they do not feel like going outside, once they are there they usually find something to do and end up not wanting to come back in.

Let kids fall and scrape their knees. Worse things have happened. Like *not* ever falling and scraping one's knees. Lady Allen of Hurtwood, a prominent British children's advocate of the twentieth century, has been credited for coining the phrase "Better a broken bone than a broken spirit."[19] It captures perfectly the two risks weighed in the conundrum, "To play, or not to play?"

I knew already in my little three-year-old heart that what I feared the most was not the angry rooster and his talons but the possibility of losing my freedom to roam and play as I pleased on the farm. I was busy exercising my free will, and to do it when no adult was looking was my favorite thing.

I learned to stay away from the rooster by my own experience, not because someone told me. I learned about what was dangerous and what was not on my own. In short, I learned about risk assessment. Crossing the stream on slippery rocks sometimes meant wet shoes and socks. Taking an unknown path sometimes got me lost. But far more often I found my way. I credit so much of my confidence as an adult to these opportunities for making my own choices out in nature—a nature that is there for us to enjoy, for our benefit, not to be shut out.

I will be forever grateful for the adults in my life who never restrained me in my wanderings and play outdoors. We may not be able to re-create such childhoods for this generation, but we can do better than we currently are without risking children's lives. In fact, if we don't, then we are in a way risking their lives.

Notes

1. Dennis Cauchon, "Childhood Pastimes Are Increasingly Moving Indoors," USAToday.com, June 26, 2007, http://www.usatoday.com/educate/college/education/articles/20050717.htm.

2. Romina M. Barros, "Daily School Recess Improves Classroom Behavior," Albert Einstein College of Medicine, January 26, 1999, http://www.einstein.yu.edu/home/news.asp?id=293.

3. Nancy M. Wells, "At Home with Nature: Effects of 'Greenness' on Children's Cognitive Functioning." Cornell University: Gannett Health Services, November 6, 2000, http://www.gannett.cornell.edu/cms/pdf/upload/Wells-2000.pdf.

4. "Lack of Outdoor Play Is Health Time Bomb for Children," The European Food Information Council (EUFIC), accessed December 23, 2011, http://www.eufic.org/page/en/show/latest-science-news/fftid/physical-activity-children-obesity/.

5. "Millions of U.S. Children Low in Vitamin D," Albert Einstein College of Medicine, August 3, 2009, http://www.einstein.yu.edu/home/news.asp?id=392.

6. Ibid.

7. Ibid.

8. "The Decline of Walking and Bicycling," SafeRoutesInfo.org, accessed December 23, 2011, http://guide.saferoutesinfo.org/introduction/the_decline_of_walking_and_bicycling.cfm.

9. Hillary L. Burdette and Robert C. Whitaker, "Resurrecting Free Play in Young Children: Looking Beyond Fitness and Fatness to Attention, Affiliation, and Affect," *Archives of Pediatrics and Adolescent Medicine* 159, no. 1 (2005): 46–50, doi:10.1001/archpedi.159.1.46.

10. Ibid.

11. Romina M. Barros, "Daily School Recess Improves Classroom Behavior," Albert Einstein College of Medicine, January 26, 1999, http://www.einstein.yu.edu/home/news.asp?id=293.

12. Ibid.

13. Nancy M. Wells, "At Home with Nature: Effects of 'Greenness' on Children's Cognitive Functioning," Cornell University: Gannett Health Services, November 6, 2000, http://www.gannett.cornell.edu/cms/pdf/upload/Wells-2000.pdf.

14. Rhonda Clements, "An Investigation of the Status of Outdoor Play," *Contemporary Issues in Early Childhood* 5, no. 1 (2004): 68, doi:10.2304/ciec.2004.5.1.10.

15. Andrea F. Taylor, Frances E. Kuo, and William C. Sullivan,

"Views of Nature and Self-Discipline: Evidence from Inner City Children," *Journal of Environmental Psychology* 22, no. 1–2 (June 11, 2001): 49–63, doi:10.1006/jevp.2001.0241.

16. Frances E. Kuo and Andrea F. Taylor, "A Potential Natural Treatment for Attention-Deficit/Hyperactivity Disorder: Evidence from a National Study," *American Journal of Public Health* 94, no. 9 (September 1, 2004): 1580–86, doi:10.2105 /AJPH.94.9.1580.

17. Howard Frumkin, "Beyond Toxicity Human Health and the Natural Environment," *American Journal of Preventive Medicine* 20, no. 3 (2001): 234–40.

18. Stephen R. Kellert, *Building for Life: Designing and Understanding the Human-nature Connection* (Washington, DC: Island Press, 2005).

19. "Better a Broken Bone than a Broken Spirit," PlayWales.uk.org, accessed March 20, 2012, http://www.playwales.org.uk/down-loaddoc.asp?id=156&page=422&skin=0.

OBJECTIFICATION AND SEXUALIZATION

"A sex symbol becomes a thing. I just hate to be a thing."

Marilyn Monroe

OUR SOCIETY IS ONE OBSESSED WITH SEX AND LOOKS. We see the objectification of women everywhere. There is no escaping it entirely. It has been this way for many decades, but the sexualization of young girls in our entertainment, media, and marketing, as well as the marketing of goods to young girls that have to do with sexuality or looking sexy, is rapidly increasing.[1]

Our own first daughter was born in 2004, and that same year I strolled through an aisle of toys with my little baby daughter snapped into the front of the shopping cart and first laid eyes on a Bratz doll. I stopped and stared in horror at the product before me. *Surely no parent in their right mind will ever buy such a thing for their child!* I thought. But as soon as I thought it, I knew that I was wrong, because we live in a "market it and it will sell" kind of society. I also realized that despite the shock and horror that I (and likely others) felt at first seeing these dolls, it would diminish over time as consumers got used to this toy and gradually became desensitized to it, just like we have become desensitized to so many other undesirable aspects of our media and marketing.

In case you are not familiar with the Bratz dolls, I will give you a brief description. First, the name is disturbing enough—or attractive enough, according to some marketing executive—but the naughty name is ameliorated (or made more disturbing, depending on one's viewpoint) by an angel's halo over the official logo. Bratz dolls are ten inches tall (an inch and a half shorter than Barbie) with an enlarged head; skinny body; huge, half-closed eyes with a sultry gaze; lots of makeup; large, pouty lips; and hardly any nose. Their dress brings Britney Spears to mind—miniskirts; bare midriffs; fishnet hose, tall, leather boots; feather boas; and so forth. Indeed, they look like little prostitutes with only the pimp missing.

I vowed right then and there that no Bratz product would ever enter our home even if it were a gift from the king of Sweden. And to make good on that vow, I have had reason to confiscate a lunch bag, a pair of pajamas, and a coloring book that have been given to our girls over the years since then. When going bicycle shopping a few years ago, the otherwise best bike in the lineup was adorned with Bratz dolls on the center bar.

I wonder how the makers and marketers of the Bratz products can sleep at night. But when considering the sales figures, I imagine that any twinge of conscience they may have ever had has long since been lulled away by the rocking of soft ocean waves against the bows of their luxury yachts. Because in 2006 Bratz dolls had already captured 40 percent of the fashion-doll market, only five years after they were initially introduced, and in 2005 their global sales equalled two billion dollars.[2]

What can I say? Sexy sells. We've known this for a long time. We see it in all kinds of marketing—commercials for cars, beer, cigarettes, perfume, clothing, household goods, food—apparently any product can be given solid sales numbers if a lightly clad or seductive woman is made part of the ad.

But Bratz dolls are intended to be a *toy* and are therefore marketed to *children*. The target audience is four to eight years old![3] The American Psychological Association (APA) noted that "Bratz girls are marketed in bikinis, sitting in a hot tub, mixing drinks, and standing around, while the 'Boyz' play guitar and stand with their surf boards, poised for action."[4] And other franchises have followed, trying to imitate the Bratz dolls, such as Trollz and Pussycat Dolls.

I do not mean to say that the Bratz doll is the cause for our sexualized society. It is of course but a symptom, albeit a severe one. The pressure of looking attractive begins young and comes from all angles, and a girl can hardly enter pre-K without in some way or another associating her worth with how she looks. I sometimes worry a bit about the effects of our "princess" culture too, where toddlers and preschoolers are groomed to base their value on their looks, their clothes (dresses), and whether the prince will want to marry them.

Of course I want my girls to know that they are beautiful, but I do not want them to measure their worth by it. And I certainly don't want them to associate their value with how sexy they are or how closely they measure up to the ideals of beauty and body image presented by mainstream media.

I am thankful for a mother who rarely commented on my looks but who nevertheless took an active interest in *me*. My own experience in life has taught me when girls have their self-worth and self-confidence disproportionately tied up in their looks, as opposed to their personality and their abilities, they will inevitably find themselves unhappy, because beauty is not constant and the ideals presented in media are impossible to achieve and maintain. And that is the point; for women to spend as much money as we do each year on makeup, clothes, hair styling, and other related products, we must constantly be chasing that impossible ideal and compete with other women in the process.

But how can we teach our daughters that being healthy, kind, honest, and hardworking are the characteristics to strive for when the celebration of being beautiful, skinny, and sexy is so loud and unrelenting around us? Probably the best and easiest way to prevent our daughters from developing a skewed and one-dimensional view of themselves is to simply turn off the TV and monitor their other media consumption carefully. The *Report of the APA Task Force on the Sexualization of Girls* claims, "Girls and young women who more frequently consume or engage with mainstream media content offer stronger endorsement of sexual stereotypes that depict women as sexual objects . . . [and] place appearance and physical attractiveness at the center of women's value."[5]

Jean Kilbourne, EdD, award-winning author, speaker, and filmmaker who has educated the public about the use of women in advertising for four decades, said in her latest film, *Killing Us Softly 4: Advertising's Image of Women*, "Girls tend to feel fine about themselves when they are eight, nine and ten years old. But they hit adolescence and they hit a wall, and certainly part of this wall is this emphasis on physical perfection." She goes on to describe not only that images created for the purpose of advertising are computer-enhanced to perfection (even when the female subject spent hours in a hair and makeup chair) but also that often photos of several different women are combined and used for a single image, all for the purpose of creating the perfect woman.[6]

"Failure is inevitable," says Kilbourne, "because the

ideal is based on absolute flawlessness. She never has any lines or wrinkles, she certainly has no scars nor blemishes, indeed she has no *pores*."[7]

Another aspect of marketing is the use of women's body parts disconnected from their persona. We have all seen the dismembered pieces or zoomed areas of women's bodies—legs, thighs, stomachs, breasts—that are used as backdrops for product placement or brand logos, usually with lustrous and glowing skin and always impossibly thin. Often when the whole body is used in an ad, the head is chopped or the face is concealed in some way. Jean Kilbourne points out that this dehumanizing of women's bodies is doing nothing to help the widespread violence against women—on the contrary.

"Turning a human being into a thing," she says, "is almost always the first step toward justifying violence against that person."

Moreover, research links sexualization with three of the most common mental health problems of girls and women—namely, eating disorders, low self-esteem, and depression.[8]

We know that the objectification of women does not just affect women. It also affects men. And it certainly affects impressionable and growing boys who are learning to become men. It hardly comes as a surprise to learn that "young boys also pick up on sexualization and appearance-based objectification of girls early by learning to sexually harass and objectify girls."[9] It is every mother's and father's desire, I hope, to raise their son to become a gentleman, someone who is respectful and kind to everyone, who knows how to treat women well and who can recognize a good woman. But if the onslaught of media is not curtailed in the home and if the inappropriate images of women are not specifically explained to the young man as being offensive and why, which lesson is he most likely to internalize?

Our society needs good role models, badly. Thankfully, there are some out there. My husband is one. He has a habit (one that he exhibited long before we had children) of turning magazines over while waiting in line at the grocery store if the cover sports an indecent or otherwise objectifying picture of a woman. By his example, our son has learned to do the same. Most of the time this works well, but sometimes the full-page ad on the back page is equally offensive or worse, necessitating the grabbing of another magazine with more benign images to cover the offensive one. Whenever I see our son go to flip a magazine, I silently pray for an M&M ad on the back (as long as the red M&Ms don't bully the others)—a nice, round primary-colored piece of chocolate with arms and legs. In that moment I say to heck with resisting the marketing of candy—my son is learning the value of decency, and he recognizes objectification as an evil to avoid.

The objectification of women can and does affect how men of all ages and life stages view women. Studies have shown how "exposure to narrow ideals of female sexual attractiveness may make it difficult for some men to find an 'acceptable' partner or to fully enjoy intimacy with a female partner"—which will provide a real hurdle for achieving a well-adjusted family life.[10] So, it not only contributes to the unhappiness of the individual but also can be counted as one of the detrimental effects on the fabric of our society as a whole by how it can weaken marriages.

Anyone who has gone shopping for a girl can attest to how difficult it is to find modest and appropriate clothing these days and how prevalent sexualized clothing is becoming, even for young girls. Take for example the mini-short with writing—any writing—across the butt ("flirt," "juicy," and "kiss" are all real examples). Now, I happen to believe that many of these clothing items are inappropriate no matter what the age of the woman, but they are 100 percent out of place on a rack of clothes for girls who will not hit puberty for several years and who should be blissfully unaware of sexiness. But *tween* (seven- to twelve-year-olds—also known as middle *childhood*) seems to be the new *teen* for fashion designers and marketers.

Indeed, researchers have noted that "the thong, an item of clothing based on what a stripper might wear, is now offered in 'tween' stores as well as children's wear departments, often with decorations that will specifically appeal to children."[11] And parents buy the stuff! Or else these products would disappear. We may lament the nature of some commercial enterprises, but we ultimately vote for our favorite products with our dollars.

I was raised with what I consider a mostly healthy attitude toward my own and others' bodies. One aspect of this that is foreign to most Americans is the laissez-faire attitude toward what I call non-sexual nudity that Swedes traditionally have held. Little children run around naked on public beaches. One summer in Sweden, my own American son froze when his six-year-old female friend stripped out of every shred of clothing right next to him so she could get into her swimsuit. I realized then that he may speak Swedish fluently, but culturally he is certainly an American.

I wouldn't have batted an eyelid at the same incident as a child, because we all did this, and not just the kids. We knew what male and female parts looked like for young and old alike. But with the increasing reports about sexual abuse, rape, and other sex crimes, there is far less room for nudity in our society that does not feel charged—especially when content once considered pornographic pushes its way into mainstream media. Hence, non-sexual nudity is becoming less common, even among children, because we know that somewhere there may be some adult who has conjured a picture in their mind of a child's body as an object of sexual desire.

A ten-year-old boy was visiting our house one day, and all the kids gathered in the kitchen to eat ice pops. So that our four-year-old would not spill her purple ice pop on her white T-shirt, I pulled it off while she ate. The visiting boy looked away, embarrassed, and explained that he had been taught not to look at women's naked bodies. I commended him for that commitment and told him this was a good thing. But then I said, "I can't know for certain, but I don't think this is the sort of thing your parents have warned against. She's just a little girl."

The result of our sexualized culture is that what was entirely non-sexual nudity twenty-five years ago has suddenly become uncomfortable. And when all nudity, even children's, is potentially sexual, curiosity and distorted views about the human body increase. The opportunity for simply learning about the body in a non-sexual way is difficult to come by. And the source from which my generation of Swedes received the first lessons about *normal* bodies is gradually being replaced by Internet searches, which will yield twisted views every time.

I am not in any way suggesting that the Scandinavian nudity attitude of my childhood be adopted as some standard. I only want to make the point that if children do not have opportunities to learn about human bodies in a non-sexual way, how can we expect them to develop a healthy understanding about their bodies? How do we expect them to satisfy the curiosity that they will undoubtedly have concerning bodies and human sexuality without running into pornography? Today's children will not be protected from nudity, mind you—it is all around us, and it is *very* sexual and objectified. What they will be hard-pressed to find is any sort of neutrality in the learning process. If we as parents would like to present curious children with facts about bodies and an attitude that is vastly different from the one the world is presenting, how do we do it? I haven't found a clear answer. I do know that the lines of communication regarding human body functions, sex, attraction, and appropriate versus inappropriate behavior need to be open and unashamed. And human body illustrations in encyclopedias and biology books are *not* condemned in our house.

One of many signs of what kids actually internalize is the self-objectification that especially girls engage in. In fact, "one study of ninth- and tenth-grade girls showed that most girls, regardless of race, engaged in self-objectification."[12] And it bears pointing out that just because a girl or a woman voluntarily objectifies herself does not mean that she is necessarily exercising her free will and choice. Perhaps she has been conditioned through countless and relentless media messages to think of herself in this way so that by the time she engages in this self-objectification it is a rather subconscious act. Only by explicit education can we hope to help her.

"If girls purchase (or ask their parents to purchase) products and clothes designed to make them look physically appealing and sexy, and if they style their identities after the sexy celebrities who populate their cultural landscape, they are, in effect, sexualizing themselves," reports the APA. "Girls also sexualize themselves when they think of themselves in objectified terms. Psychological researchers have identified self-objectification as a key process whereby girls learn to think of and treat their own bodies as objects of others' desires."[13]

While we teach the growing generation about the inappropriateness of objectification and sexualization, we are also tasked with the challenge of teaching them that sex is not bad in and of itself but that there is a time and a place for it. Our sexuality is a gift that when properly used will strengthen marriage and make our lives happier. Surely this is a message we want to teach. Research has shown that "sexual well-being is an important part of healthy development and overall well-being, yet evidence suggests that the sexualization of girls has negative consequences in terms of girls' ability to develop healthy sexuality."[14]

Too many girls think of and treat their own bodies as objects for others' desires. They may not see what they are doing, but we as adults can often spot it. Take, for example, the sort of pictures girls upload of themselves on the Internet. Even teens who are not sexually active will often upload self-objectified pictures to social media sites. These are often staged, self-taken pictures with sultry expressions and provocative poses. Often the kinds of pictures that generate many "positive" comments from peers, such as "Hot!" and "Sexy!," also add fuel to the fire. And the trend is spreading to the younger ages as more and more young kids spend time online and have social media profiles.

Says the APA, "Younger girls imbued with adult sexuality may seem sexually appealing, and this may suggest their sexual availability and status as appropriate sexual objects" which should be cause for serious alarm for all parents, because any sexual object runs the risk of becoming a victim.

Since this chapter is more about sounding the alarm rather than discussing methods, I would refer parents to *So Sexy So Soon: The New Sexualized Childhood and What Parents Can Do to Protect Their Kids* by Jean Kilbourne and Diane E. Levin. It is an excellent and eye-opening resource for today's parents.

I wish to end on a more positive note. I was part of a wonderful nonfiction book club before the birth of my fourth child and commencing my graduate studies. During our discussion of the book *Born to Buy: The Commercialized Child and the New Consumer Culture* by Julie B. Schor, one of the women expressed something I have often thought about since. This particular mom is an unabashed left-wing, liberal feminist, and her words were in essence, "I have realized that we liberals have much more in common with very politically conservative parents than either of the political parties would like us to think. Feminists and liberals have long objected to the sexualized culture we live in and the way women are portrayed in media, and both groups make efforts to deal with this onslaught. Very conservative families generally feel the same way. They come at the issue from perhaps another angle, but they have the same concerns. We really should learn to cooperate better on the things we agree on."

And it is absolutely true. The Venn diagram of left- and right-wing politics intersects at least two-thirds of the way, probably more, when it comes to our sexualized society, making it one of the most agreed-upon subjects in all of politics. It seems this would be an excellent place to not only foster political unity and bipartisanship, but also gain some ground in the fight for a happier society and a healthier childhood for our precious ones.

Notes

1. *Report of the APA Task Force on the Sexualization of Girls*, American Psychological Association, 2007, http://www.apa.org /pi/women/programs/girls/report.aspx.
2. Margaret Talbot, "Little Hotties," NewAmerica.net, December 5, 2006, http://www.newamerica.net/publications /articles/2006/little_hotties_4487.
3. *Report of the APA Task Force on the Sexualization of Girls*, American Psychological Association, 2010, http://www.apa.org /pi/women/programs/girls/report-full.pdf.

4. Ibid.
5. Ibid.
6. *Killing Us Softly 4: Advertising's Image of Women*, directed by Jean Kilbourne (Northampton, MA: Media Education Foundation, 2010), DVD.
7. Ibid.
8. *Report of the APA Task Force on the Sexualization of Girls*, American Psychological Association, 2010, http://www.apa.org /pi/women/programs/girls/report-full.pdf.
9. *Beauty at Any Cost: The Consequences of America's Beauty Obsession on Women and Girls* (Washington, DC: YWCA, 2008).
10. *Report of the APA Task Force on the Sexualization of Girls*, American Psychological Association, 2007, http://www.apa.org /pi/women/programs/girls/report.aspx.
11. Ibid.
12. *Report of the APA Task Force on the Sexualization of Girls*, American Psychological Association, 2007, http://www.apa.org /pi/women/programs/girls/report.aspx.
13. Ibid.
14. Ibid.

TOXICITY

"Our contemporary culture, primed by population growth and driven by technology, has created problems of environmental degradation that directly affect all of our senses: noise, odors, and toxins which bring physical pain and suffering, and ugliness, barrenness, and homogeneity of experience which bring emotional and psychological suffering and emptiness. In short, we are jeopardizing our human qualities by pursuing technology as an end rather than as a means. Too often we have failed to ask two necessary questions: First, what human purpose will a given technology or development serve? Second, what human and environmental effects will it have?"[1]

United States, Report of the Subcommittee
on Air and Water Pollution (7 Aug. 1969)

I HAVE WANTED TO FOCUS THIS BOOK ON THE TWENTY-first-century parent's circle of influence, but with this chapter we are entering a realm where parents can have only a partial impact. Still, I feel I must address this, because increased awareness is the first step, and with it we can help bring about changes in the long term.

It has been widely understood that children are more susceptible than adults to certain chemicals and toxins. In addition, children's exposure to chemicals "in foods and in the environment are different and often greater" compared to adults.[2] Their developing bodies and central nervous systems are more vulnerable. Their diet consists of more of certain foods, and they drink more liquids and breathe more air proportionate to their body weight than do adults. Children also crawl on the floor and ground outside and often put their fingers in their mouths. In short, they are, compared to adults, "more exposed to potentially harmful pollutants."[3]

Such as with many ills in our society, toxicity has been on the rise for decades. Scientists from the School of Hygiene and Public Health at Johns Hopkins University reported that from "the mid-1960s to 1980, pesticide use sharply increased from 400 million pounds to more than 800 million pounds per year—an increase largely driven by the development and use of chemical herbicides in agriculture." By 2001 the figure had reached 1.2 billion pounds of pesticides sprayed per year in the United States, and there are claims that "less than 0.01 percent of all those billions of pounds that are sprayed actually make it to the intended pest!"[4]

Is it any wonder, then, that chemicals are found in our ground water, our streams and lakes, our soil, our food, and our bodies? And further, how can any one of us think even for a moment that we are not negatively affected by this as a species?

Children cannot even enter this world without already being exposed to harmful substances. Toxic chemicals and metals do cross the placenta. That pure, undefiled being lying in your arms hours after birth already has an average of more than 230 dangerous chemicals in her blood.[5] In fact, levels of toxic metals are often higher in infants than in maternal blood.[6] Exposure to vehicle exhaust fumes in the womb has been associated with lower IQ at age five. And out of the 80,000 chemicals that are used in the United States, the Environmental Protection Agency (EPA) has only tested 200. Out of those, only 5 have had restrictions put on them.[7] In addition, toxins such as mercury and organochlorine compounds that mothers are exposed to reach infants in significant amounts through breastfeeding.[8]

Mothers-to-be can do much to ensure a healthier pregnancy. They can eat a healthy diet and take prenatal vitamins. They can exercise and avoid smoking cigarettes as well as inhaling secondhand smoke. They can avoid drinking alcohol. They can choose "green" and natural household products in their homes. They can eat organic (if they can afford it). They can join the "No-Poo" movement (like my passionate sister, Daniella—and by the way, this movement is a lot more comprehensive a lifestyle than just discontinuing the use of shampoo).

But even with concerted effort it is impossible to fully protect our unborn babies or ourselves from toxic chemicals that we inevitably come in contact with, unknowingly, in our everyday lives. We have to breathe, after all. The old adage "What you don't know, can't hurt you" is certainly false in this case.

We are exposed to so many toxins every day, including PBDEs (polybrominated diphenyl ethers, or flame retardants), in computers, food, lead, clothes, bottle tops, hard plastics, hygiene and beauty products, water repellents, electronics, nonstick products, food packaging, carpeting, cleaning products, furniture, phthalates, children's toys, and cosmetics—in addition to the "traditional" air, water, and ground pollution.

New research is emerging that suggests more and more ways we humans are affected by living in a toxic world. But we have only scratched the surface. A study published in 2010 in the journal *Pediatrics* claims association between exposure to pesticides with cases of attention deficit/hyperactivity disorder (ADHD) in the United States and Canada. While no doubt this disorder has many and varying causes, this study is compelling. The research team collected urine samples of 1,139 children ages eight to fifteen and analyzed the samples for levels of pesticide residue. Those with higher urinary levels of breakdown products of organophosphate pesticides were also the ones with the highest rates of ADHD. The article states that "children with levels higher than the median of detectable concentrations had twice the odds of ADHD . . . compared with children with undetectable levels."[9]

Time magazine reports that organophosphates work by causing damage to the nerve connections of the brain and that this is how they actually kill agricultural pests. "The chemical works by disrupting a specific neurotransmitter, acetylcholinesterase, a defect that has been implicated in children diagnosed with ADHD."[10]

This information can make parents feel helpless. It does me. Especially since this is but the tip of the iceberg of related studies of health issues linked to environmental toxins. It is true that we come in contact with chemicals through so many sources in our everyday lives. But, as the researchers who worked on the aforementioned study suggest, parents can do some things like avoiding the use of "bug spray in their home[s] and [trying to] feed their children organically grown fruits and vegetables, if possible."[11]

Philip Landrigan, MD, MSc, professor and chair of the Department of Community and Preventive Medicine at Mount Sinai School of Medicine in New York and known for his many decades of work in protecting children against environmental threats to health, says, speaking of pesticides,

"For most people, diet is the predominant source. It's been shown that people who switch to an organic diet knock down the levels of pesticide by-products in their urine by 85 to 90 percent."[12]

But organic food is not cheap and is not always easy to come by unless we shop at specialty stores and frequent the farmers' market. I do not shop organic most of the time because of the need for short-term savings and for keeping the food budget in check to feed a large family—you know, like getting through the week on last week's paycheck. The price difference between regular flour and organic flour, for instance, is more than double! I like to bake my own bread (love my bread machine) for the great taste as well as to avoid the many additives and unnecessary ingredients in store-bought bread. But it becomes cost-prohibitive to try to bake with organic flour. Still, as often as I feel I can, I buy *something* organic just to make my voice heard. Organic apples, potatoes, and carrots, and some organic cereals, are often reasonably priced, so I usually buy those. It is my vote with my few dollars to let the market know that I care, that I want more organic products, and that I would like them to be more affordable. But organic strawberries are often three or four times the price of pesticide-sprayed ones, so unless they come from our own garden or from a local grower at the farmers' market (who doesn't spray, even if he is not certified organic) my family is not likely to eat non-sprayed strawberries anytime soon.

I think with longing and respect of my deceased grandfather, Hans-Eric, who, through the 1960s to 1990s, farmed organically. I remember flowers growing around the fields and how neighbors and competitors mocked him. I recall the discussions at the large dining room table, where a mix of family members and farmhands drank their ten-o'clock coffee and had their 3:00 p.m. dinner. I saw my grandfather sprinkle flaxseed on top of his own organically grown muesli with buttermilk, tapping open his own boiled organic egg with his spoon and lecturing on the ills of pesticides and his distaste for artificial fertilizer.

"Who do they think they are killing with that stuff?" he would say about those *other farmers.* "Insects, weeds, or themselves?" The answer was in the question. And I believed him, of course, because he was my grandfather and I loved him. Now I agree because I know he was right.

The Environmental Working Group (EWG) has released what it calls its Dirty Dozen—a list of the worst contaminated fruits and vegetables, where apples, celery, and strawberries top the list.[13]

But beware that processed foods are often worse than fresh produce when it comes to pesticide levels. They often contain genetically engineered corn and soy, both of which have been manipulated to withstand more and higher levels of insecticide spraying—a practice which is backfiring since it has led to so-called superweeds.[14] And if you think eating meat is any better, please consider the accumulation of toxins that occur when first an animal eats the contaminated food (often engineered corn) and then we consume the animal. And that is to say nothing of the cancer-causing nitrites and other preservatives and treatments added to so many meat products.

In December 2010, major news organizations all over the United States, including the *Washington Post*, reported on the findings of the EWG after surveying the drinking water in thirty-five American cities looking for hexavalent chromium (sometimes called chromium-6), a known carcinogen.[15] This chemical is also known as the "Erin Brockovich chemical," whose persona and city—Hinkley, California—were made infamous in the year 2000 movie starring Julia Roberts. Thirty-one of the cities tested by the

EWG (89 percent) were found to have hexavalent chromium present in their drinking water.[16]

There is no federally mandated upper limit for this chemical in drinking water, but the state of California has sought to set a limit on chromium-6 as a "public health goal" for safe levels of "0.06 parts per billion (ppb) to reduce cancer risk."[17] No other state in the union has such a limit, despite the fact that many cities across the United States have, independent of the EWG, identified high levels of this carcinogen in its water supply, Chicago, Illinois; Milwaukee, Wisconsin; and Cameron, Missouri, being among them.[18]

Among the thirty-one cities found to have hexavalent chromium in their drinking water, twenty-five of the cities had levels which exceeded the proposed California limit.[19] The EWG concludes, "At least 74 million Americans in 42 states drink chromium-polluted tap water, much of it likely in the cancer-causing hexavalent form. Given the scope of exposure and the magnitude of the potential risk, EWG believes the EPA [Environmental Protection Agency] should move expeditiously to establish a legal limit for chromium-6 and require public water suppliers to test for it."[20]

Perhaps some will shrug their shoulders and say that these are trace amounts and that since we are exposed to so many different things, how can we possibly keep up? Well, one of the thirty-one cities tested had a chromium-6 level of 12.9 parts per billion, which exceeds the proposed California limit by *two hundred times*! That city is Norman, Oklahoma—the family-friendly university town where my husband and I have raised our children. This was the drinking water I consumed during four pregnancies. Yes, it is personal to me.

"But your kids have been okay," a friend from out-of-state said to me when discussing this issue. "They are all healthy."

To which I responded, "For now."

Philip Landrigan testified before the Committee on Environment and Public Works in the United States on October 1, 2002. He called for "design policies that will protect children against environmental toxins and will allow our children to grow, develop, and reach maturity without incurring neurologic impairment, immune dysfunction, reproductive damage, or increased risk of cancer as a consequence of toxic environmental exposures."[21]

He explained, "Children are undergoing rapid growth and development, and their developmental processes are easily disrupted. Since children have more future years of life than most adults, they have more time to develop chronic diseases that may be triggered by early exposures."

Citing a study done in Connecticut, Landrigan explained that "85 to 90 percent of school districts" in that state routinely used pesticides without any apparent need. "Pesticides used indoors included bendiocarb, chlorpyrifos, cyfluthrin, cypermethrin, pyrethrin, piperonyl butoxide, tralomethrin, and bromadiolone." Don't know what those are? Except for pyrethrin, neither do I, but I am pretty confident I don't want any child of mine breathing or touching any one of them. But apparently the use of pesticides inside schools and on school grounds is extremely common.

Dr. Landrigan points out that "the effects of pesticide poisoning on children can be acute and obvious, or chronic, cumulative, and subtle." So how is a parent to know if an illness their child has can be traced back to chemical exposure in their everyday life? Could it be that my daughter Elina's asthma is a result of harmful substances she has inhaled throughout her childhood? It may be impossible to draw such individualized conclusions. But we can certainly take note of the statistical increase in children's health issues, the dramatic rise in pesticide use in our country—pesticides that we know can cause these health issues—and conclude that the risk is not worth taking. And it affects all of us to one degree or another, regardless of where we live or what our socioeconomic status.

Landrigan concluded his testimony by saying, "Hundreds of new chemicals are developed every year and released into the environment, and many of these chemicals are untested for their toxic effects on children. Thus, the extent of children's exposures to environmental chemicals will almost certainly continue to increase: the problem is not going away." He said those words ten years ago, and as I write this, the problem has not gone away; it has grown.

Not surprisingly, there was an outcry among the residents of Norman, Oklahoma, when the report about our drinking water came out. Concerned citizens turned to their mayor and city council to demand filtering and other protective measures. My own husband corresponded with the mayor and city council members via email and was disappointed with their replies. Though the mayor did commission a working group of council members to look into the issue, one council member pointed out, "Please note that the recommended levels of maximum exposure is based on 40–70 year periods, so the time we spend will not have an appreciable impact." This tells me the council does not take the threat very seriously. The mayor herself said, "I would caution citizens to not overreact," and, "I reassure you that Norman's water meets all regulatory standards." Yes, because where chromium-6 is concerned, there *are no* regulatory standards!

In the following weeks and months, leaflets were sent out to the households of Norman, stating in big, bold letters, "Norman's water is safe to drink!" This rhetoric is all based on the absence of laws and on what we *don't* know, and frankly ignores many things we *do* know. The chemicals and health risk correlation is, in my mind, far too alarming to ignore or to say "we don't know enough" to pursue aggressive legislation that will protect current and coming generations. It is irresponsible in the extreme for community leaders to dig and find every shred of evidence that may support doing nothing in the face of a real threat, just to prove their good political record. Sadly, this seems to be the norm rather than the exception. Chemicals and toxins are indeed innocent until proven guilty. And to prove them guilty beyond reasonable doubt means that incalculable lives must first be tragically impacted. We only have to look to DDT and lead to see this precedent.

I also think of the precedent set with cigarette companies and how difficult it was to "prove" that tobacco causes cancer, let alone to get the CEOs of tobacco companies to admit any such thing. It became a game in the courts driven by potential sales revenue to be earned or lost, even though everyday citizens could see through the charades but were still powerless to change anything.

But cigarettes are different. Though highly addictive and harmful, we can choose to smoke or not to smoke (presuming we can resist the aggressive advertising and avoid secondhand smoke). If we are informed about the truth of their health impact, we can arm ourselves with that information and choose not to buy a package when we are in the store. We can choose not to be exposed to secondhand smoke (unless we are a child in the presence of caregivers who smoke). But we cannot choose to avoid harmful chemicals altogether. Legislation is the only thing that can effectively provide lasting change in this area.

It is my prayer that parents not be silent on this matter and that together we can make a real and lasting change before more tragic changes are done to our children's and our own bodies.

Notes

1. United States Environmental Protection Agency, "Environmental Quality: Summary and Discussion of Major Provisions," *Report of the Subcommittee on Air and Water Pollution* (7 Aug. 1969), Legal Compilation, Jan. 1973, Water, vol. 3, 1365, http://nepis .epa.gov/Exe/ZyPURL.cgi?Dockey=20015B5S.txt.

2. Lynn R. Goldman and Sudha Koduru, "Chemicals in the Environment and Developmental Toxicity to Children: A Public Health and Policy Perspective," *Environmental Health Perspectives* 108, no. 3 (June 2000): 443–48.

3. Ibid.

4. Walter Crinnion, "Pesticide Loss: A Massive Public Health Issue," *Huffington Post*, May 18, 2010, http://www.huffington post.com/dr-walter-crinnion/environmental-health-pest_b _572187.html.

5. "Toxic Childhood," in *Toxic America, Toxic Childhood*, transcript, CNN, June 3, 2010.

6. B. Windham, "Effects of Toxic Metals on Learning Ability and Behavior," Florida League of Conservation Voters Education Fund, accessed January 22, 2012, http://www.flcv.com/tmlbn .html.

7. "Toxic Childhood," in *Toxic America, Toxic Childhood*, transcript, CNN, June 3, 2010.

8. B. Windham, "Effects of Toxic Metals on Learning Ability and Behavior," Florida League of Conservation Voters Education Fund, accessed January 22, 2012, http://www.flcv.com/tmlbn .html.

9. Maryse F. Bouchard, David C. Bellinger, Robert O. Wright, and Marc G. Weisskopf, "Attention-Deficit/Hyperactivity Disorder and Urinary Metabolites of Organophosphate Pesticides," *Pediatrics* 125, no. 6 (June 1, 2010): 1270–77, doi: 10.1542 /peds.2009-3058.

10. Alice Park, "Study Links ADHD in Kids to Pesticide Exposure," Time.com, May 17, 2010, http://www.time.com/time/health /article/0,8599,1989564,00.htm.

11. Ibid.

12. Leah Zerbe, "Pesticides in Food Linked to ADHD in Kids," MSNBC.com, September 11, 2011, http://www.msnbc.msn

.com/id/44260583/ns/health-childrens_health/t/pesticides
-food-linked-adhd-kids/.

13. "EWG's Shopper's Guide to Pesticides," Environmental
Working Group, accessed January 22, 2012, http://www.ewg
.org/foodnews/summary/.

14. Leah Zerbe, "Pesticides in Food Linked to ADHD in Kids,"
MSNBC.com, September 11, 2011, http://www.msnbc.msn
.com/id/44260583/ns/health-childrens_health/t/pesticides
-food-linked-adhd-kids/.

15. "Chromium-6 Is Widespread in US Tap Water," Environmental
Working Group, December 2010, http://www.ewg.org
/chromium6-in-tap-water.

16. Lyndsey Layton, "Probable Carcinogen Hexavalent Chromium
Found in Drinking Water of 31 U.S. Cities," *Washington Post*,
December 19, 2010, http://www.washingtonpost.com/wp-dyn
/content/article/2010/12/18/AR2010121802810.html.

17. "Chromium-6 Is Widespread in US Tap Water," Environmental
Working Group, December 2010, http://www.ewg.org
/chromium6-in-tap-water.

18. *Wikipedia*, s.v. "Hexavalent Chromium," accessed January 20,
2012, http://en.wikipedia.org/wiki/Hexavalent_chromium.

19. "Chromium-6 Is Widespread in US Tap Water," Environmental
Working Group, December 2010, http://www.ewg.org
/chromium6-in-tap-water.

20. Ibid.

21. *Environmental Threats to Children's Health in America's Schools:
The Case for Prevention* (2002) (testimony of Philip J. Landrigan).

LEGO AND
BLOCK PLAY

"If you were to take a saw, cut my head open and look at my brain, all you would see is LEGO blocks."

Isak Fisher

I F YOU HAVE A SON OVER THE AGE OF FIVE, CHANCES ARE you know more about LEGO than a pregnant woman knows about morning sickness. Our own son discovered the wonders of LEGO at age five on an eight-hour flight from Chicago to Copenhagen, Denmark. He had played with LEGO blocks before, of course, but only with the kind that comes in an assortment of a variety of colors and sizes in a bucket; never before had he used step-by-step instructions.

I had the . . . ahem . . . *pleasure* of flying with my three children, ages five, four, and ten months. The "fasten seat-belt" sign was of course on, but try telling that to a baby. I was keenly aware of her screams, but several passengers in front of me thought they would be helpful by turning and looking at me disdainfully, as if that would give me the proper clue to try and quiet my child. Four-year-old Elina had already spilled her crayons all over the floor, and I tried to retrieve some of them while also reaching for the sippy cup and sandwich that Anja had rejected in her fury of being strapped in her seat. I was, in other words, the picture of serene motherhood.

In all honesty, I repress the memory of these flights until travel becomes imminent again and I need to retrieve some basic traveling tips from the hidden stores of my memory. I can say, for example, that the last time I went back to Sweden, Julia cried for seven out of the seven hours and forty minutes our flight lasted, but I relate it in a detached sort of way. The full recollection never presents itself until I am actually on a plane again and about to take off. But I digress.

About an hour into this Chicago–Copenhagen flight, I suddenly felt a tap on my right shoulder, and I turned to pay attention to my hitherto completely quiet son.

"Look, Mom! I made this!" he said and held up a LEGO racecar. In front of him on the fold-down tray lay the plastic bag the pieces had come in along with the instructions.

"That's fantastic! But where did it come from?" I wondered.

"The airplane lady gave it to me," he explained happily.

Bless Scandinavian Airlines! I thought to myself (and wondered whether they also might have some secret Danish sleeping pills I could give to Anja).

Isak then spent the remainder of the flight disassembling and rebuilding his new LEGO car and playing with it in between. I only had to rescue fallen pieces half a dozen times. I suppose it is fitting, in a way, that he was filled with this new love and passion for LEGO as he stepped onto the tarmac in Denmark, of all places. And to think that this interest was so forceful even before he knew that LEGO was married to his existing passion, namely *Star Wars*. It didn't take him long to make that discovery, however.

On his sixth birthday a few months later, there was a clear theme, one that has remained fairly consistent for birthdays and Christmases ever since. And the passion for LEGO shows no signs of letting up—now spanning half the duration of his existence on earth. And although the LEGO collection has gotten rather large over the years, that first yellow-and-red racecar from his transatlantic flight sits in a place of honor in his bookshelf even as I write this.

I do not own stock in the LEGO company. (I wish! Alas, it is privately owned.) That is not why I write this chapter. I do it because LEGO has been such a huge part of my parenting experience (and I know that I am in good company in this regard) and because of the many developmental benefits of not just LEGO blocks but also building blocks in general. I have met few children who do not like to sit down and build when blocks are placed in front of them. Our little Julia caught on early, building with Duplo (the larger, toddler-size LEGO blocks) and showing some intelligent design behind her constructions at a year old.

Whether or not a three-year-old can make a tower of nine or more building blocks is actually used by pediatricians as a gross motor skills and hand-eye coordination milestone marker. And it is a sign of cognitive and social development if he or she can cooperate with a peer in stacking blocks.[1]

Parents have observed the benefits of building with blocks (not just LEGO blocks) for a long time. And research supports this. Studies have found that children build foundational math skills through play, including "counting, equality, addition and subtraction, planning, patterns, classification, volume and area, and measurement." When children have informal comprehension of these concepts, they provide the reference on which they later build formal mathematics.[2]

Another study has linked plentiful preschool block play with advanced math skills in high school.[3] After controlling for IQ, gender, and socioeconomic status, researchers found that out of the thirty-seven preschoolers tested, those who obtained a high block performance score had a higher correlation of advanced math performance in high school. Interestingly enough, there was no difference noted in third and fifth grade, but by seventh grade, *one* of the measures (standardized test scores) began to go up. By the end of high school, all four areas of measurement (number of math courses, number of honors courses, advanced math courses taken, and grades) showed that the children who had played extensively with building blocks as young children had superior math skills to those who played less, little, or not at all.

The researchers explain why this is: "Construction play with blocks offers the preschool child the opportunity to classify, measure, order, count, use fractions, and become aware of depth, width, length, symmetry, shape, and space; thus, one can make a direct relationship with the skills acquired in block play as being foundational for the later cognitive structures."[4]

But block play is not just good for mathematical skills; it has been associated with improved language as well. In another study of children ages eighteen to thirty months from middle- and low-income families, researchers found that when they distributed two sets of building blocks to their families, it "was associated with significantly higher language scores" six months later, compared to the control group.[5] Add to that a diminished tendency for watching TV, and I think it is safe to say that block play is a good thing. The basis for this research was the many other documented benefits of parents sitting down to play with their children in an era when more and more parents rely on so-called educational television for their children, even though the latter has been associated with delayed development.[6]

The researchers explain that "through play, that is, unstructured manipulation of objects, the child begins to develop a mental picture of and cognitive categories about the objects around him or her," which is a foundational step in developing memory, impulse control, understanding of object permanence, attention span, and language.[7] The greatest gain in language development happens when parents engage with their children, providing so-called scaffolding around the child's existing abilities.

"Should we put the red block here?" (points to the block in question)

"No! Dis one!"

"Oh, you want the big blue one instead. Go ahead."

As children grow, they begin to create stories and fantasy settings for their play, which is key in developing executive functions—those much-talked-about abilities to plan and carry out, correct and solve. There is no need to elaborate on why these skills are crucial for a successful life. Suffice it to say that limited executive functions can lead to especially poor decision making in the teen years, when humans are generally vulnerable to poor judgment anyway. Unfortunately, some reports in the media and among researchers, as well as observations made by seasoned teachers, suggest these executive functions may be in decline among many of today's children. One of the ways to foster this development is through block play. Isn't it great when solutions to, or at least prevention of, potentially big problems can be so simple?

Other very encouraging research regards the benefits of LEGO blocks to children with autism. This will probably not be news to parents of children with autism spectrum disorder (ASD), who are usually extremely well-educated about this universe, but for the benefit of the rest of "parentdom," I am including it here.

During a three-year study of ASD children focused on long-term outcome, children who received so-called LEGO therapy were compared to a control group who participated in comparable non-LEGO therapy. Two outcome measures were used, the Vineland Adaptive Behavior Scale socialization domain and the Gilliam Autism Rating Scale social interaction subscale. On both of these measures, both groups improved. The LEGO therapy group made more significant gains, however, compared with the control group, in overall social competence as well as decreased autistic behaviors.[8]

Another study over high-functioning children with ASD ages six to eleven received similar results.[9] Some of the reasons that LEGO therapy is so successful for children with ASD are thought to be that LEGO play capitalizes on their inherent strengths, providing a solid foundation for the therapy to work. Children with ASD are therefore more likely to participate in those behaviors that are challenging to them—namely, imaginative play and social interaction—because they have an interest and a talent for the base activity.

LEGO has become a genius of a marketing machine, joining with well-loved children's brands, which makes the toys irresistible. The recent push for making more girl-friendly sets has been received with enthusiasm in our household, though LEGO has perhaps rightfully been criticized for not developing enough gender-neutral sets. And if I may, I'd like to address just a few areas that I am not thrilled about when it comes to LEGO.

First, it is pricey! Especially the "name brand" sets. One of our children's generous uncles sent a fifty-dollar gift card at ToysRUs for each of the kids for Christmas one year. The girls shopped several items and had balances remaining on their cards until June. Isak bought his desired LEGO set, which depleted the card, and he still had to add five dollars to cover the sales tax.

In the early part of Isak's LEGO career, he was especially fond of working to earn money to buy certain sets. We paid him a dollar per job, such as vacuuming the living room or sweeping the driveway. After having earned enough to buy two twenty-dollar LEGO sets, he desperately wanted a set that cost thirty-four dollars. After sighing and fretting over the prospect of having to do so many jobs, he suddenly perked up.

He said, "Mom, I have the solution! Instead of paying me one dollar per job, you could pay me ten!"

To which I replied, "That, my son, would require much bigger jobs or a different employer."

The good news is that in order to access the developmental benefits of playing with LEGO blocks, you do not have to spend a ton of money. Boxes of assorted pieces are less expensive than the high-profile sets, and many times they can be found used in perfectly good condition at garage sales, at thrift stores, or on Craigslist for very little money.

Another concern is simply a matter of logistics. With younger siblings in the house, LEGO pieces require careful supervision and storage out of reach so they do not end up in baby's mouth. And those of us who have stepped on LEGO pieces know how painful that is, so cleaning up after each play session is a good idea all around.

My third and biggest issue is the marketing of adult heroes and movies to young children. *Star Wars* is tricky. The first three movies made are not as intense as the last three, making them more appropriate (if not entirely) for younger kids. The newer ones, especially *Revenge of the Sith*, with its PG-13 rating, are not suited for children. Yet many of the LEGO sets marketed to seven-year-olds depict characters and scenes from these movies.

There are also LEGO sets of *Indiana Jones*, *Prince of Persia*, and *Pirates of the Caribbean*, none of which are children's movies. The building sets are fine and child appropriate in my opinion. It is the source I take issue with. It becomes a chore for parents to resist children's demands to see the movies, and it blurs the line between what is for kids and what is not when *Pirates of the Caribbean* sets are right next to *Toy Story* and *Cars*. A child will reasonably believe that the movies are for them. LEGO is by no means alone in this kind of marketing, nor is it the worst example. Other toys and Halloween costumes for small children are based on these same characters and others of even more questionable appropriateness for kids. It becomes a parent's job to resist this push, as always, because it is important to remember which movies are designed for children and which are not. Even if kids play with toys and LEGO sets, it does not mean they should automatically watch the movies. We don't expect a first grader to be able to do eighth-grade math, right? Neither should we excuse ourselves into thinking that a young child "can handle" movies made for adults.

Having said that, I am still a LEGO fan. And I do look forward to the day in the future when, thanks to the meticulous safekeeping of my son, we will be able to sell some of his then-out-of-production sets on eBay to pay for college. No, what am I saying? I don't look forward to that at all. I want him to stay little a good while longer, building and playing with his LEGO sets on the dining-room table.

Notes
1. "Developmental Milestones Record—3 Years," Medline Plus, April 19, 2010, http://www.nlm.nih.gov/medlineplus/ency /article/002014.htm.
2. Patricia O'Hara, Diane Demarest, and Harriet Shaklee, "Early Math Skills—Building Blocks for Idaho's Future," Thurston Early Childhood Coalition: Block Fest, November 2005, http://

www.blockfestwa.org/downloads/BFWhitePaper.pdf.

3. Charles S. Wolfgang, Laura L. Stannard, and Ithel Jones, "Block Play Performance among Preschoolers as a Predictor of Later School Achievement in Mathematics," *Journal of Research in Childhood Education* 15, no. 2 (2001): 173–80, doi:10.1080/02568540109594958.

4. Ibid.

5. Dimitri A. Christakis, Frederick J. Zimmerman, and Michelle M. Garrison, "Effect of Block Play on Language Acquisition and Attention in Toddlers: A Pilot Randomized Controlled Trial," *Archives of Pediatrics and Adolescent Medicine*, October 2007, http://archpedi.ama-assn.org/cgi/reprint/161/10/967.pdf.

6. Ibid.

7. Ibid.

8. Daniel B. Legoff and Michael Sherman, "Long-term Outcome of Social Skills Intervention Based on Interactive LEGO© Play," *Autism* 10, no. 4 (2006): 317–29, doi:10.1177/1362361306064403.

9. Gina Owens, Yael Granader, Ayla Humphrey, and Simon Baron-Cohen, "LEGO® Therapy and the Social Use of Language Programme: An Evaluation of Two Social Skills Interventions for Children with High Functioning Autism and Asperger Syndrome," *Journal of Autism and Developmental Disorders* 38, no. 10 (2008): 1944–57.

BOARD GAMES

"Those who know the marvels of chess and wonder why this game of all games does not enjoy greater popularity may also ask why Pepsi-Cola is consumed by more people than Chateau Lafite, or the Beatles are more familiar than Beethoven."

Gregor Piatigorsky

HERE IS A BRIEF WORD ON BOARD GAMES. THEY COMprise one tested and proven face-to-face alternative to virtual forms of entertainment. These days we often have to make that concerted effort to steer children toward more traditional forms of fun. My definition of board games includes any game that is played with real, tangible pieces, face-to-face, even if a board is not necessarily used. Card games and tile-laying games are great too, and very portable.

Board games generally don't cost very much, yet they can provide hours of entertainment. And most of these games are great for cognitive and social development. Some games even help increase children's deductive reasoning and problem solving. Another plus is that from about age four, pretty much all ages can play together, depending on the game. Mixed ages and genders do not matter. In fact, multiple ages can often enrich the game and provide balance in cases of feelings hurt from losing. An adult presence can often keep cheating in check as well.

Learning to be a good loser is a crucial lesson that board game players learn early. Many parents have made the mistake of letting a young child win a few too many times, depriving them of the opportunity to truly learn to lose (so as not to throw a fit when playing with peers). We've made that mistake with our children. At first, I think our motivation might have been to make them feel good about themselves and for them to learn to like playing the game. But such a strategy backfires quickly. Think about it; as much as winning is focused upon in our culture, the truth is that we will experience losing far more often and will only rarely find ourselves in first place.

There are scores of different types of board games. Some are team games (like Pictionary), some involve strategy (like Clue and Monopoly), and some do not require taking turns but rather everyone plays simultaneously (like Bananagrams). Mancala games (Kalah being the one I played as a child) are some of the simplest and oldest games played around the world. And they are great for keeping basic math muscles fit. Our toddlers have always loved the battery-operated fishing games (with the gaping plastic fish that the player hooks on a plastic fishing rod). Hungry, Hungry Hippos is another good toddler-friendly game.

Some games (even if they involve die-casting and counting, which are good preschool skills) are based on luck, like Candyland. I can honestly say that even when my kids love it, I barely *endure* it. For family game night to be successful, I don't think it is too much to ask that parents should enjoy the games too. Chutes and Ladders is a better game for five-year-olds, in my opinion. It helps kindergartners get a good grasp of the number line, and my kids have really enjoyed it.

In general, I much prefer games that involve some sort of cooperation, strategy, or planning. Mancala, Connect Four, Mastermind, Monopoly, and Clue are all examples of games that require strategy. Clue involves deductive logic. Tic-tac-toe is fun, simple, yet challenging. I prefer playing with moveable pieces on a nine-square board rather than with pen and paper. I have often managed to keep a game going with a child at the kitchen bar while cooking dinner. But the pen-and-paper version is a happy alternative to an electronic game when waiting in the doctor's office, for example.

Monopoly can be used to teach simplified financial principles. I know it had a big impact on me when I was young. The thought of mortgaging a property has always had a negative connotation for me because of that game. As a mom, I rarely have the time to sit down for a game of Monopoly with the kids. (I mean, what parent does? It can take three days!) The Monopoly Junior version has therefore been a lifesaver, with its snappy thirty-minute rounds. It is one of my family's favorite games.

One thing parents can do to improve the cognitive and academic value of games they play is to ask their children to explain their thinking. Children tend to not explain themselves nor ask their opponent to do so, even when they play on the same team and cooperate.[1] It doesn't require much extra effort to do this, but it can really improve the quality of the experience from a learning perspective. The kid in question probably won't even notice that you are doing it. After all, games are played, first and foremost, because they are fun, not because of their developmental and educational value. But the latter is undeniably a nice side effect.

I have some fond childhood memories of playing games. My dad taught me to play a seven-card, two-player game called Cucumber, which often entertained us on early weekend afternoons in our summer cottage (before 5:00 p.m., when there was no programming on the two TV stations we had to choose from). I recall playing cards a lot, and several of my earliest memories involve observing adult family members engaged in card games in the evenings, with much laughter and hilarity. There is the oft-related tale of me, at age three, sneaking up behind my mom as she was winning and declaring to the other players (my mom's parents) that "Mom has Grandpa Hans-Eric in her cards." He was known for his rather long beard and looked much like the king of hearts in that particular deck.

One of the best bits of concrete knowledge I ever gained from a game was African geography. I have retained most of it, which is more than I can say for some of the other continents that I merely studied and tested on in my school career. This was thanks to my favorite board game, called The Star of Africa. The board was the map of the African continent, and markers were placed upside down on major cities. On one of those markers was the largest diamond in the world, also known as the Star of Africa, and the object was to find it first and then bring it to either Tangier or Cairo before one of your opponents obtained a visa and beat you to it. Along the way (players choose their own path), one could count on running into more precious gems, pirates, and robbers. I still remember not being able to hold back the tears when I was playing against my grandmother and I lost all my money *and* my accumulated jewels in Addis Ababa.

That particular game was purged from the evidence of my childhood long before I left home, so imagine my joy when my mother bought a new one for our family not long ago. Our children are now well on their way to becoming savvy in African geography.

To spice things up a bit, we've hosted board game

afternoons at our house from time to time. We usually plan for two thirty-minute games and a snack. It seems to be just enough for a successful little event. Occasionally some tears and cries of cheating have arisen, but this is just par for the course when learning about rule following, fair and unfair playing, problem solving, and friendship. Those lessons cannot be practiced while engaged in a screen game, so when it happens, I remind myself that it is a sign of progress!

Chess, one of the oldest board games, equally loved or hated, it seems, has not lost popularity. It is a favorite among the boys who come to our house. Albert Einstein was an avid chess player and supposedly said, "Chess grips its exponent, shackling the mind and brain so that the inner freedom and independence of even the strongest character cannot remain unaffected."

There is a sense of timelessness when one sits down to play chess. The game has been played for literally ages. And multiple studies show that playing chess helps improve both verbal and mathematical abilities among schoolchildren, and the frequent playing of chess has long been associated with higher IQ.[2] For this and other reasons, chess is in some places a school subject in its own right.

We got our son a chess computer for his birthday one year, which in many ways defeats the whole face-to-face interactive purpose of board games (as opposed to hand-held and video games). I bought it in part, I suppose, to dull my guilty conscience for not having enough time to sit down and play with my son. But it is not completely without interactive value, I suppose. The chess computer talks like a mad, medieval knight, and sometimes the kids like to try an illegal move just to hear the knight rattle his sword and cry, "I will not cheat, for I will not permit cheating!"

Notes

1. Gwen Dewar, "Board Games for Kids: Do They Have Educational Benefits?," Parenting Science, 2009, accessed January 23, 2012, http://www.parentingscience.com/board-games-for-kids.html.
2. Aleksandr Kitsis, "Benefits of Chess for Academic Performance and Creative Thinking," Vivacity, accessed January 23, 2012, http://www.vivacityinc.com/chess/Articles/BenefitsOfChess.pdf.

SPECIAL NEEDS

"I know God will not give me anything I can't handle. I just wish He didn't trust me so much."

Mother Teresa

MORE THAN IN PAST GENERATIONS, WE HEAR THE term *special needs*. And for good reason. The number of children with special needs is increasing. Considering the many and different types of needs—emotional, developmental, as well as medical and health issues—few be the families that go unaffected. And if one family is spared, they know someone who is not.

Regardless of potential misdiagnoses, or overdiagnoses, right now, in every community, families are dealing with the realities of issues such as attention deficit/hyperactivity disorder, learning disabilities, autism spectrum disorders, sensory processing disorder, anxiety disorders, obsessive-compulsive disorders, seasonal allergies, asthma, food allergies, lactose intolerance, celiac disease, gluten intolerance, and the list goes on and on. Those of us who will graduate parenthood and go on to become grandparents can expect to have at least one grandchild with some special need or another.

This is not intended to be a comprehensive overview of

the many issues parents can be faced with under the label "special needs," just as this book does not begin to cover all the aspects of twenty-first-century parenting. Nor is this a manual for how to deal with them. This is but a cursory glance at the reality and prevalence of special needs, as well as a call for compassion—on ourselves, our struggling neighbors, and others we come in contact with.

New research is emerging as to the origins of special needs and health issues. Some studies point to causes stemming from living in an increasingly toxic society and how this is impacting human health in general and children's health specifically. I touched on some of this in the toxicity chapter. But this little chapter will not deal with the potential causes for special needs, even though it is crucial that we find out. This is a two-front war: addressing the causes on one hand, and treating and handling special needs as they manifest themselves on the other. And for many of us, the handling portion is quite enough. It is something we cannot leave to others or shirk until another day.

Suffice it to say that special needs children are many, and caring for them can bring extra challenges on top of what is already a daunting task. In fact, special needs are frequently the source of much heartache and worry, not to mention financially challenging. For example, parents of a child with autism spectrum disorder (ASD) can expect to spend 4.1 to 6.2 times more in medical costs than they would for a child without ASD.[1]

In our little family of four children, we deal with seasonal allergies, asthma, epilepsy, sensory processing, and anxiety. Many in our circle of friends deal with the same, but adding to that list, we have oppositional defiance disorder, attention deficit/hyperactivity disorder, autism, Asperger's, speech impairment, celiac disease, nut allergy, hearing loss, Down syndrome, and diabetes.

In our children's school, many children have a life-threatening peanut allergy, necessitating completely nut-free classrooms and nut-free tables in the cafeteria. Sometimes when I think about the fact that several of these children are so sensitive they cannot even have peanut traces touch their skin, I get light-headed. What is it like, I wonder, to be a parent and send your kindergartner to school, knowing that they have this life-threatening allergy, and trust that he or she will not come in contact with a smudge left behind on some surface or on the fingers of one of the dozens of children who brought peanut butter and jelly sandwiches for lunch that day?

Special needs are all around us. Schools are making accommodations and adjustments to see to the growing number of children whose needs have gone unmet in the past, but not nearly fast enough.

According to the Center for Disease Control and Prevention (CDC), "Approximately 13% of children have a developmental disability, ranging from mild disabilities such as speech and language impairments to serious developmental disabilities, such as intellectual disabilities, cerebral palsy, and autism."[2] And 41 percent of children with a developmental disability have multiple disabilities. One definition of developmental disabilities (DDs) describes them as being "chronic physical, cognitive, speech or language, psychological, or self-care conditions that typically originate during childhood; are likely to continue indefinitely; and require additional coordinated services, support, or other assistance for an extended duration or during a lifetime."[3]

And speaking of lifetime needs, the US Census Bureau released numbers saying that one in five Americans reported some level of disability in 2005, amounting to 54.4 million Americans, or "roughly equal to the combined total populations of California and Florida."[4] The number increased by 3.2 million from 2002, the previous time the US Census Bureau collected such information (and has not declined since). Out of these, 16 million people were classified as having difficulty with cognitive, mental, or emotional functioning. Of children ages six to fourteen, 7 percent, or 2.5 million, have trouble doing regular schoolwork.

I am so glad for increased awareness, help, resources, and understanding for special needs—not just for parents whose children are affected, but also for people in general, because we all live in communities and need to work together.

The many issues and principles presented in this book do, for the most part, apply equally to children with and without special needs. Hours and hours of playing video games, for example, and a lack of outdoor play is not really good for any child, unaffected or affected by special needs. Better nutrition benefits everyone, and so on. In fact, the ills of twenty-first-century parenting often do greater harm to children with special needs than they do to others. Special needs children are many times in extra need of wholesome activities and a less virtual childhood.

Thankfully, in our family none of the needs are severe, except perhaps the case of epilepsy, since the seizures can be life-threatening. Still, we have to deal with many of these needs every day, and some days are better than others. The world can be such a harsh and unforgiving place, and as a mother, I hope to focus on ways my children can be equipped to face the realities of the world rather than the other way around. I think this is something that can be reasonably done when your children's needs are *not* severe.

When special needs *are* severe, the full arsenal of help and accommodations needs to be used, and dealing with those needs becomes a lifestyle in its own right. Indeed, such families often find their entire outlook on life changing, viewing the world through a different lens than before. Some of us can lay this chapter aside after reading it and go about our business. When we do, I hope we will remember that in our schools, our neighborhoods, and our country, millions of families cannot lay it aside, even for a day.

I'd like to end this chapter by pointing out that children, when they relate to one another, often manage to look beyond the special needs and see the person, the soul. One poignant example of this was when our daughter Elina had a friend who couldn't talk. Or so she told us one day when we were discussing what "mute" meant. She had just turned five.

"I have a friend like that," she said simply.

"You do? Who?"

"Annie, my best friend at school," she replied.

"Annie, whom you have played with *every day* this year?"

"Yes."

"She is mute? She can't *talk*?"

"Yes, Mom, she is mute. She can't talk."

I quizzed her over the next several days to know just exactly what she meant by saying that Annie couldn't talk. Elina had *never* mentioned this before, and she had played with Annie daily at school since three weeks into the fall semester. At the first parent-teacher conference, the teacher went on and on about how grateful she was to Elina for being shy Annie's friend. She said Elina always included Annie in the girl's group play and made sure she had a place among them, Elina being one of the leaders in the class and *the* authority on flying Pegasus games. I was thrilled to hear it, but I did not understand the extent of Annie's shyness— nor that it wasn't shyness at all that she suffered from.

Over the course of a week after the "mute" discussion,

the description slowly emerged. But only because I asked twenty different questions. To Elina it was nothing remarkable.

"Annie doesn't talk, but she can play. She can make an angry or a happy face. And she can sometimes whisper in my ear, but not since I came back from Sweden."

We took a trip to Sweden for three weeks that year, in February and March, and the teacher was relieved when Elina finally returned to school, because Annie had been rather forlorn without her friend. But again, I had not understood just how much.

My thoughts went back to the first three weeks of school, before Elina had discovered Annie as a playmate. I always walked Elina to the classroom, and Annie was the only one who cried at drop-off—and miserably too. But these kids are only four when pre-K begins, so having a few criers per class is not unheard of. Suddenly, I realized her crying stopped just about the time that Elina dubbed Annie her best friend.

I asked the teacher about it finally, because I was so puzzled about Annie's lack of words, and even more that I had only learned about it after eight months of school. She confirmed it but could not elaborate because of FERPA (Family Education Rights and Privacy Act).[5] The explanation finally came from Annie's mother.

Annie was not mute but suffered from selective mutism.[6] Although she chattered away without pausing for breath at home with her mom, dad, and sister, Annie clammed up in any public setting, including school, and did not even speak to or around her grandparents anymore. The condition was worsening, which explained Elina's statement about Annie not having spoken since she returned from Sweden. And for the whole school year, Annie had spoken to only one person: Elina. And only in whispers in Elina's ear. Elina had been the translator, for lack of a better expression, for Annie at school. Annie answered no direct questions unless they could be responded to with a head shake, with a nod, by pointing or some other gesture, or by whispering in Elina's ear so she could say it for her.

I asked Annie, shortly thereafter, at drop-off one morning if she wanted to come to our house for a playdate later that week. She smiled widely and nodded while holding Elina's hand, her large, brown eyes glittering with excitement, like any five-year-old's would. That night I asked Elina again:

"So, since we came home from Sweden, Annie has not whispered in your ear?"

"Only once," said Elina.

"And what did she say?" I pressed.

Elina cupped her hand over her mouth to illustrate, then said in a whisper, "You are still my best friend."

That is *all* Annie spoke to Elina the last eight weeks of school, even though they played together every day. That is *all* she said in school, period, the last eleven weeks. It was, to this date, the last thing Annie ever said to Elina. But despite all of that, Elina and Annie managed to not just play but also become consumed in their fantasy worlds of flying horses and other characters. They sat next to one another every day, they colored, they played with Play-Doh, they cut with scissors and glued. They ran with smiles to meet each other each morning, and Annie listened patiently to anything and everything Elina had to say, which, I am sure, was not a little.

How? I suppose because they are children and they have a far more malleable manner in which they relate to others. There was a meeting of the souls there that mattered more than Annie's selective mutism. In fact, it mattered so little that Elina never once thought to even mention it at home for eight months, even though she often related the different games they played at recess and described the classroom activity centers they had chosen each day. Elina became a fiercely loyal friend and received a friendship back that was truly beyond words and certainly beyond special needs.

Notes

1. "Autism Spectrum Disorders (ASDs): Data and Statistics," Centers for Disease Control and Prevention, May 13, 2010, http://www.cdc.gov/ncbddd/autism/data.html.
2. Ibid.
3. S. L. Boulet, C. A. Boyle, and L. A. Schieve, "Health Care Use and Health and Functional Impact of Developmental Disabilities among US Children, 1997–2005," *Archives of Pediatrics and Adolescent Medicine* 163, no. 1 (January 1, 2009): 19–26, doi:10.1001/archpediatrics.2008.506.
4. US Census Bureau Newsroom, "Number of Americans with a Disability Reaches 54.4 Million," news release, December 18, 2008, http://www.census.gov/newsroom/releases/archives/income_wealth/cb08-185.html.
5. "FERPA for Students," US Department of Education, accessed January 6, 2012, http://www2.ed.gov/policy/gen/guid/fpco/ferpa/students.html.
6. For more information, visit www.selectivemutism.org.

LINE UPON LINE

"What saves a man is to take a step. Then another step."

C. S. Lewis

PARENTING CAN SEEM OVERWHELMING IF WE DON'T remember to do it just one step at a time, one day at a time. We won't cure all our weaknesses today or tomorrow, nor will we be able to help improve on all the needed aspects of our children's development this week. Raising children is done one hour at a time over thousands of hours.

As wonderful, sweet, and smart as our children are, my husband and I agree that there is at least one area in which our kids display a distinct and obvious weakness. It is probably due to the quality of their parenting (or lack thereof). For all our parental efforts at achieving reverence during church, we have not seen the amount of fruit that we had hoped to reap. This lack of reverence in church has caused me some consternation, because their behavior has not just been the commonly seen wiggles to be expected at young ages.

On a Sunday not too long ago, we were jammed rather tightly together in a short pew, and I thought to myself that the close quarters provided far too much *touching* for this to be a peaceful church service for our family. To my delight and surprise, the kids behaved calmly. Our two oldest sat bent over a nature book one of them had brought, and in whispers, they discussed the animals and the habitats for most of the service. The youngest two were engaged in coloring quietly without so much as throwing a crayon.

As I sat there taking in the peaceful scene, it occurred to me that the two oldest should not be reading a nature book but something more religious, or better yet, they should pay attention to the speaker. Well, that last part was probably too much to ask, I quickly concluded, but I reached into my bag to pull out one of the many fun and engaging religious materials for children I always pack so I could exchange it for the nature book they were reading. But at that moment, I heard the words in my mind: "Precept upon precept, line upon line," and I stopped what I was doing.[1] This was clearly a day to celebrate how appropriately they behaved in church rather than an opportunity for improvement on church reading materials. Rome was not built in a day. What they needed to hear from me that day was lavish praise on what they were doing *right* and not a syllable uttered on what could be improved. Oh, how I need to take that lesson to heart every day!

Russian psychologist Lev Vygotsky (1896–1934) has become something of an education guru. One of the many terms we can thank him for is the *zone of proximal development* (ZPD). The ZPD is, in essence, the distance between what a child (or learner) is capable of on their own and what they are capable of with help from a teacher or more capable peer.[2]

A simple example can be a child learning to ride a bicycle. She may wiggle and wobble unsteadily on her own, making it impossible for her to perform the task. But if someone holds her steady, she can practice her balance and her pedaling. Gradually, she will need less and less support, perhaps needing only the occasional steadying as she takes a turn, until she eventually can do it on her own. Riding her bike independently was thus within her zone of proximal development, and with some help she closed the gap.

Parents generally understand this principle even if they have never heard of Lev Vygotsky. They would not try to teach a two-year-old to ride a bicycle, for example, because it is so obviously without the child's reach to learn it at that age. But many other aspects of raising children are more nuanced, and it behooves us to take a step back, evaluate what we can reasonably expect our children to do (which is a highly individualized judgment), and then provide the necessary support for them to succeed at their level. As in my example above, it was not yet in my children's ZPD to sit reverently looking at church materials. It was, however, in their ZPD to sit quietly and look at something of their interest.

Mornings and evenings can be major stressors in our household. Getting four kids out the door—on time, fed, dressed, and groomed, with their teeth brushed and lunches packed and without any bickering between them or nagging on my part—was at one point proving nearly impossible.

They are perfectly capable, I thought to myself when I pondered a solution. *I should not have to remind them of every step.* The answer came in the form of written "scaffolding." Having a list of the expected evening and morning to-dos and a place to check them off made all the difference. It kept them on track to complete the tasks within the time allotted. As I write this, I could probably remove the scaffolding, meaning I could probably take down the lists, because they have memorized them. But I would rather not give a loophole for excuses, if you know what I mean.

A related educational theory comes from Stephen Krashen, a linguist and educational researcher. His "input hypothesis" has greatly influenced second-language education in this country and others. He basically argues that in order for a learner to move to the next level in language proficiency, he must receive what Krashen calls "comprehensible input." Perhaps you have heard some who argue that the best way for non-English students to learn English is to simply immerse them in an English-speaking school (also known as the sink-or-swim method). Well, research does not support this as the fastest or best way to learn (V. Collier, J. Cummins, F. Genesee, S. Krashen, D. Short). It is slow, and by the time students have acquired English, they are so far behind academically that they often drop out of school. So when teaching a student (and making use of their own language is not a possibility), the way to help them is to provide "comprehensible input" that is slightly above the student's current level of competence that they can still understand.[3] In this way, grade-level academic content can be taught, using simplified language and scaffolding, at the same time as developing language skills.

Parents do this naturally when speaking to their toddlers, for example. They do not use their newscaster vocabulary and phrasing. They modify their language using simple words, short phrases, gestures, and other scaffolding to make sure the little one understands. And in this way children climb the ladder one rung at a time in their language development. This principle can be translated to almost any parenting activity. We tailor our instruction and our dealings to be just slightly above the child's current level of competence, hoping to be able to raise their abilities one level at a time. It does not require monumental effort every day. But consistent effort will pay off, a little at a time.

But some days I am just too tired to uphold the high

standards I set for myself. Or perhaps I just prefer being lazy. It is human nature, right? Why else would it be so much easier to spend an hour surfing the web than an hour exercising? Perhaps the same reason it is so much easier to get kids to eat macaroni and cheese than vegetable soup. It certainly is tempting to order pizza and serve it to a happy crowd rather than slave over the stove preparing a healthy and well-balanced meal to a complaining crowd.

It is at least ten times simpler (not to mention faster) to clean the playroom by myself than to get the kids to do it (although it is getting better!). And it is much easier to turn on a favorite DVD than to engage everyone in an activity that may require refereeing at some point (and cleanup). It is also a lot less work to just *buy* that desired toy rather than make the child work and earn the money. Why? Because the latter option includes teaching the jobs that need to be done, performing quality control, and putting up with potential complaining from the precious laborer in the process.

Perhaps when religions speak of the straight and narrow path to God versus the broad way of the world, the meaning is at least in part concerned with this same idea of how easy it is and in how many ways we can corrupt ourselves into becoming lesser creatures on the path of least resistance, rather than becoming the fully developed, more noble human beings that we are capable of being when we discipline ourselves just a little. There are two kinds of pain, I've been told: the pain of discipline and the pain of regret.

The facts and principles presented in this book are not meant to be overwhelming. They are actually quite simple: more outdoor play (more play *period*), less television, fewer video games, less computer time, more sleep, more human interaction, better nutrition, and some basic money management skills will make this generation of children healthier and happier now and as adults. Having more balanced kids will also make parents less frazzled. But it does require pushing back against the fierce stream of media messages that would influence us, and our children, to act and to think differently.

And if I fail at swimming upstream sometimes, I try not to despair. Instead, I keep in mind that there are other issues far more important where my efforts should not fail. Even if I fall short in many other respects.

Do they know how precious they are? Can they hear—through the din of sometimes stressed interaction, direction-giving, and nagging about cleaning their messes, doing their homework, and *please* not pestering their siblings or destroying the house—how absolutely *wonderful* they are? Do they know that there is not a single thing they need to do better or differently to capture more of my love?

These may be my number-one recurring questions and worries. They cause that feeling of regret that lodges itself in my chest some nights after they are in bed, usually after a long day (with little sleep the night before) that left me weary and impatient from errands, chores, homework (theirs and mine), sibling quarrels, making dinner, and more chores. Another day gone of their childhood! The race to adulthood is relentless.

Thankfully, if I ever forget to tell them, they remind me. I'll hear a voice calling me from one of the rooms after bedtime.

"Mom! You forgot to tell me that I am the best nine-year-old in the whole world!"

I love it when they do that. These are not empty words to them, after all—even though I repeat them every night with only slight variations. It has been many years now since we settled the question, "But what about the other kids in the world that are not in our family? What if some of them are the best kids in the whole world?"

"Their moms and dads think they are," I admitted.

"But what if they are and I'm not?"

"No, that can't be, because *I* have been given the best kids in the world. I feel it in my heart. It is the other moms' and dads' job to think that their kids are the best. But for me, there is no other *x*-year-old on the planet who I would rather have than you."

At bedtime I also try to remember at least one thing—something specific, something positive—each child did that day and to talk about that. I have a wish that all over the face of the earth, millions upon millions of little children are the best in the world to their parents. Whatever other shortcomings parents may have and however far from the ideal people's lives may be otherwise, I hope that all children are folded in the love of their own little universe. It is my wish and prayer that this love be reinforced and lodged securely in their little hearts, one day at a time, line upon line.

Notes

1. Isaiah 28:10.
2. Saul McLeod, "Zone of Proximal Development," Simply Psychology, 2010, http://www.simplypsychology.org/Zone-of-Proximal-Development.html.
3. Stephen Krashen, "Principles and Practice in Second Language Acquisition," accessed January 10, 2012, http://www.sdkrashen.com/Principles_and_Practice/index.html.

ABOUT THE AUTHOR

Victoria grew up free range in picturesque Sweden and spent lots of time with her grandparents in northern Norway. Speaking Swedish and Norwegian as a small child, she went on to learn English, Spanish, German, and Latin.

As an adventurous sixteen-year-old, she signed up for a year abroad and was placed in Wyoming. Despite thinking that she had landed on the moon, she fell in love with the people and the country.

After completing Swedish high school and a study abroad in Spain, she returned to the United States and met Mark Fisher in California. After a semester in Israel, she returned to the United States, where she married Mark. Together they have four bilingual children.

Victoria holds a bachelor of arts in letters and will soon complete a master of education in bilingual education/ teaching English as a second language.

Beginning at age six with the gruesome tale *The Teribel Dragon,* Victoria has been an avid writer across many genres all her life, with a certain weakness for all things fantasy. Her passion for parenting and public education is central in her life.

The Fishers currently reside in Norman, Oklahoma.